DATE			

SEDUCTION

A PORTRAIT
OF
ANAÏS NIN

MARGOT BETH DUXLER, PH.D.

SEDUCTION: A PORTRAIT OF ANAÏS NIN
Copyright © 2002 by Margot Beth Duxler, Ph.D.

EdgeWork Books · Boulder, CO 80302 · www.edgework.com
For orders, call 800-773-7782
Cover Design: Michael Brechner / Cypress House
Cover Illustration: "Reflections", original painting by Jessica Broitman.

Library of Congress Cataloging-in-publication Data
Duxler, Margot.
  Seduction: a portrait of Anaïs Nin / by Margot Beth Duxler. -- 1st ed.
    p. cm.
Includes bibliographical references.
  ISBN 1-931223-02-5 (casebound : alk.paper)
  1. Nin, Anaïs, 1903-1977. 2. Authors, American--20th century --Biography.
3. Diaries--Authorship --History--20th Century. 4. Women and literature
-- United States -- History -- 20th century. 5. Duxler, Margot--Friends
and associates.   I. Title.
  PS3527.I865 Z5982002
  818'.5209--dc21   2001053741
  [B]

COLOPHON

Book design by Cypress House, Fort Bragg, California.
The text face and folios are set in Mrs. Eaves, designed by Zuzana Licko.
The headings are in Alcuin, designed by Gudrun Zapf von Hesse.

2 4 6 8 9 7 5 3 1

For Michael

PERMISSIONS

Acknowledgments

⌒ Beginning at the beginning, I want to thank my teacher and friend, Lenore Borzak, who first introduced me to the work of Anaïs Nin, encouraged me, and believed in my goals and dreams. I also wish to thank Gunther Stuhlmann for opening his door to a stranger and delivering a letter and a crystal ship to Anaïs for me in the spring of 1968.

For her love, availability, patience, clinical acuity, and gift for retail therapy, I want to thank Joan Levy.

A special debt of gratitude and thanks goes to my dear friends and family who understood my need to lock myself up and write: Elena Storer and Bob Nitzberg, Bill Smith and Suzanne Shea Smith, Judy and Rodger Doty, Harriet and Rick Barone, Ina Jaffe and Lenny Kleinfeld, Heidi Chote, Geoff Velgluth and Jamie and Erin Chote-Velguth, Terry (photo-op) Lorant and Pete Jacobson, Pamela Prince, Carole Duke, Ouisue Packard and Larry Moskowitz, Jane Handel, Amy (the Dot) Wilner and Richard Kaplan, Denny and Jo Zeitlin, Vivian Dent and Don Hazen, Laurie Case and Andy Baker, Susan Boxer, Vicki Topaz, Caroline Smadja, Odile DuPont, Tobey Hiller and Phillip Zeigler, Michael Lerner and Debora Kohn, Tantele Harriet Goldman, Albert B. Katz and Matilda Woo, and Anne Bartley and Larry Mc Neil. Also, applause and thanks to new friend, artist, and cover-girl supreme, Jessica Broitman. Thanks for waiting!

To Alison Owings — editor, reader, writer, and generous soul—I owe the return of free weekends. Without her skilled eye and red pen this book would still be incomplete.

And to the bee-catcher, Marshall Bush. Thanks!

I also wish to thank Noel Riley Fitch, not only for her compassionate biography of Anaïs Nin, but for her thoughtfulness and generosity of spirit. To the women of Edgework, this book owes its being. For many hours of hand-holding I want to thank Lis Jorgens, Annie Holmes, and Constance Spheeris. This book exists because of the devoted energies of Kim Chernin and Renate Stendhal who gave substance to a vision and asked only one question, though many times repeated: If not, why not?

For good-enough mothering I wish to thank Jill Horowitz, because some good things never change.

My thanks and love to Rupert Pole, whose music, generosity, and affection over the years have been a continuous source of strength, support, and inspiration.

This book and the path my life has taken would not exist at all if not for Anaïs. My debt to her is one of gratitude, love, and thanks.

And finally, thanks to my husband, Michael Bader, who has the patience and compassion of a Buddha, for his enduring love, understanding, humor, and gift for communicating with cats.

PREFACE

WHO WAS ANAÏS?

The writer Anaïs Nin was born on February 21st, 1903 in Neuilly, France and died on January 14th, 1977 in Los Angeles, California. She wrote novels and short stories — influenced by the French surrealists — as well as essays and erotica. She is best known however, for her diaries. The first volume was published in a self-censored version in 1966 and became an immediate sensation.

Anaïs began diary writing when she was eleven years old while on a ship bound for New York after her parents separated in 1914, and her mother moved the family from Europe. Initially intended as a letter to her father, diary writing became a habit that Anaïs continued almost without interruption throughout her life.

During her life and since her death, Anaïs Nin's contribution to 20th century literature has been debated by her supporters and detractors. The edited diaries that were published during her lifetime were greeted with acclaim by critics who admired her fluid, lyrical style and psychological insight. Perhaps even more importantly, her portrayal of herself as an independent woman and writer, self-sufficient and sexually liberated, inspired a generation of women looking for guidance as they struggled with social inequities and changing mores and expectations. She became a heroine to many women who idealized her autonomy, creativity, and her relationships with such luminaries as Henry Miller, Antonin Artaud, and Otto Rank.

The success of her diaries stirred interest in her earlier works of fiction, especially the erotica that she wrote in the 1940s for a private collector. These works include *Delta of Venus* and *Little Birds*, both of which were published posthumously.

When the unedited versions of her previously published diaries were released after her death, however, great controversy about Anaïs Nin as a person and as a writer was sparked. These unexpurgated volumes presented a very different portrait from that of the free spirit of the edited tomes. The Anaïs Nin who was revealed in the posthumously published diaries was emotionally dependent on her extended family and emotionally and financially dependent on a previously unmentioned and wealthy husband. The discrepancies between who Nin was and who she presented herself to be are at the core of her life and her work.

CONTENTS

PART 1

⌒

FINDING ANAÏS

Each friend represents a world in us, a world possibly not born until they arrive, and it is only by this meeting that a new world is possible.[1]

— Anaïs Nin

⌒ I first became familiar with Anaïs Nin's work in 1968, two years after the edited volume of her diary, covering her early years in Paris (1931-1934), was published. Like many women of my generation, I was fascinated by Anaïs, who appeared to have struggled successfully with the pressures of cultural expectations and social mores, and created for herself a fulfilling, artistic life that included both work and love. She was particularly inspiring to me because her diary suggested that she had suffered from and overcome her own struggles with creativity and depression as well as external pressures from a conservative family and a patriarchal culture. Anaïs became my inspiration. Her courage gave me hope, an ideal to strive for, and a way of making meaning of my own life struggles.

In 1968 I was a twenty-year-old student attending a junior college in a suburb of Chicago. The social landscape I had been born and raised in was changing seemingly overnight. The Civil Rights movement paved the way for the women's and gay pride movements. The availability of the birth control pill was revolutionizing cultural norms vis à vis sexuality, and the Viet Nam War catalyzed anti-war activism across demographics. The protest-turned-riot during the Democratic National Convention in August of 1968 made headline news around the world when Chicago's mayor, Richard M. Daley, turned the police against the protesters, declaring their grievances illegal and effectively initiating a state of seige.

In retrospect, I can see that one of the elements that drew me so strongly to Anaïs was the need and wish for a mentor — a woman I could respect and even idealize, to help me with my own transition from youth to young adulthood. Because my own mother was so conservative, so frightened and critical of anything outside the realm of her experience as wife and mother, I could barely discuss my ideas and hopes with her, let alone expect and receive guidance. Her main focus in raising me and my younger brother was to promote my brother's independence and to instill in me the conviction that to be a worthwhile woman I must be beautiful and thin. She made it very clear to me that I would never meet any reasonable standard of beauty, but I could achieve and maintain a slender silhouette. My interests in music, writing, travel and literature were tolerated, but not taken seriously. Without irony, my mother used to tell me, "You're a nice Jewish girl. You'll get married. Have children. That's what you want. It's what all girls want." Even then I knew that she meant well. She wanted the best for me. Yet she could not see beyond her own experience and history when she imagined my future.

Therefore, she could not see me.

My father, in true post-war style, kept his distance from the female domain of house-work and child rearing, maintaining the role of bread winner and disciplinarian. He was famous in our family for his sense of humor and his temper. Good grades and good behavior were expected. Deviation from set standards was met with severe punishment. His anger was unpredictable. An off-hand comment or forgotten chore could result in bruises from a well-placed punch, yet only to me. He was never violent with my mother or brother. Years later, I speculated that I was privileged to his outbursts of violence because he and I were so similar. He saw traits in his eldest child that he could not tolerate in himself — shyness disguised as extroversion, anxiety couched in humor. Because he could not accept his own vulnerabilities, he attacked them in me.

Though at the age of twenty I did not know what I wanted to do for my life's work, my world had always been anchored in a love of language and music. I was one of those kids who can be seen walking home from school with a violin case slung across her shoulder like a quiver of arrows, her nose in a book, barely aware enough of her surroundings to keep from walking into traffic. I had played violin and viola since I was ten and kept a diary since I was eleven to help me through what I later diagnosed as depression. It was catalyzed by the loss of my family's first and last dog, a Dalmatian named Domino, whom we had to return to his kennel because of behavior problems. I began every diary entry with a kind of mantra, invoking the powers of the cosmos to make me worthy of his return. As a puppy, Domino's enthusiasm for eating dirty socks from the laundry basket and snatching everything from chicken to broccoli off the table was at worst annoying, bordering at times on cute. As he grew, however, he became more and more difficult to manage. Discipline was met with defiance, threatening growls, and increased disobedience. Neither of my parents knew much about dog training. Neither my three-year-old brother nor my eleven-year-old self could possibly have taken the lead. We needed help. When I took him for walks, I would fly down the street, holding fast to his leash as he bolted ahead. During the week days, he was left alone for far too long. To occupy himself he chewed the furniture and practiced digging techniques on the living room carpet. The more badly he behaved, the more ignorantly we punished him. He was banished to the basement for long hours or chained to a post in the back yard. My mother was frequently overwhelmed by his bad behavior and constantly threatened to give him away.

The deciding incident occurred when I came home from school one day and went to get him from his back yard prison to take him for a walk. He lunged at me with a deep, rumbling growl. I moved quickly out of range and his teeth only grazed my arm. My mother, who witnessed the incident from the living room window called my father. That night they sat me down and explained that they would have to return Domino to the kennel. In my child's heart, I knew it was my fault. I had ruined my beautiful dog I loved so much. I was convinced that if I worked relentlessly to become a better person and wrote in my diary every day to track my progress, I might once again merit Domino's return. My parents took him back to the breeder one evening while I was at a party. They were unusually understanding and kind, which ironically made me feel more blameworthy. I fell into a fierce depression that lasted for six months and manifested itself in terrible nightmares and a dread of being away from my mother. My solace was to write in my journal.

At almost twenty years old, I was still living with my parents because they had forbidden me to go away to school. The rationale for their dictum was that we could not afford out of state tuition and that they were concerned about another, but this time, diagnosed depression. This episode was prompted by my terror that my parents would discover that I was no longer a virgin. Even more critical than thinness in my mother's assumptions of qualities for being allowed to live, was the absolute expectation of virginity before marriage, and just for good measure, as long as possible afterwards. During a discussion one night after I came home from a date, I found my mother waiting up for me, darning socks and watching "A Farewell to Arms," on television. I sat with her to see the end of the movie, in which Catherine Barkley dies giving birth to a still-born child conceived out of wedlock. To my great astonishment and greater horror, at the climactic moment, my mother put down her sewing, turned to me with a frosty gaze and said, "That's what happens to women who have sex before marriage. And that's what should happen to them. If I ever found out that you weren't a virgin on your wedding day, I would commit suicide. The shame would be unbearable."

This pronouncement struck me to the core. That very night, after eighteen months of going together, my boyfriend and I finally had sex. My mother's threat confirmed my suspicions that she was, in fact, a mind-reading witch, and I would never be able to have a private life of any kind unless I managed to keep my real self hidden from her at all times.

Even as an adult, I find it stunning that I was so vulnerable to my mother's threat. At the time, neither my parents, nor I, nor the psychiatrist I was seeing, had the insight to know that the best treatment for me would have been to leave my overly controlling parents. It was not the financial burden of out of state tuition that was the problem, but rather the emotional burden of "out of sight" tuition. None of us understood the self-reinforcing effects of the situation. My parents' efforts to protect and help me only increased my dependence and helplessness.

The psychiatrist threatened to hospitalize me and tell my parents if I continued having sex with my boyfriend, so I created an alternate life I could talk to him about. Mostly, this life consisted of non-existent plans for the future, including getting married and having children — goals he could leak to my parents. In the meantime, I dreamed of my escape. Would I go to Paris and really learn the language as I had wanted to do since high-school French? Maybe New York, to study music? Or California, to write? Dreaming was an escape in itself. I became increasingly anxious that my parents would discover who I really was and that my mother actually would kill herself. I wanted to grow up, and get away, but I did not know how.

And then, in the spring of 1968, my English teacher, Lenore Borzak, intuiting my need for women with whom to identify, gave me the first published volume of Anaïs's diary, and changed the course of my life. I read the book transfixed, hopeful, with a sense of recognition and the fragile beginnings of a realization that I might be able to create a life for myself, as Anaïs had done for herself. I could dismiss convention and parental warnings and take my chances in the unknown. I felt I had found an anchor in the world outside my family in a harbor that I had never before seen, but that seemed as familiar as if it were my own home port. The depression began to lift as possibility took root and my fantasies of escape took form. I had found a woman who celebrated sensuality, creativity, inquiry, adventure. Anaïs represented everything that my parents wanted to purge from their lives and from the lives of their children.

I was naïvely determined to meet Anaïs. Having little sense of my own competence, I was quick to attribute every positive event to luck and every negative one as confirmation of my own lack of worth. So when the dean of my school purchased the Swallow Press, which published Anaïs's paperbacks, it felt as if a benevolent and personal fate had intervened on my behalf.

As it turned out, I had made plans to visit friends in New York over spring break, and the dean was happy to give me the name and address of Anaïs's agent, Gunther Stuhlmann, who lived in Greenwich Village. It was through the gatekeeper, Mr. Stuhlmann, that I thought I could reach Anaïs, via letter, gift, or some other expression of gratitude for the hope her writing had brought me. After a protracted search for an object that would properly symbolize the way in which her writing had touched me, I found what I hoped was the perfect metaphor. It was a ship made of blown glass — fragile, fanciful, a vessel for carrying dreams. I wrapped it with great care, infused as it was with my nearly desperate desire to reach her, to be seen by her. Inside the carefully packed box was a letter of thanks — a love letter really — in which I confessed my adoration and my relief at having found a maternal soul-surrogate.

I must have been afraid that if I called Mr. Stuhlmann in advance he would have turned me away. I wanted so much to believe in fate, in magic, in the rightness of my quest that I chose to take my chances and simply appear at his doorstep as quickly as the taxi from J.F.K. airport could deliver me. The afternoon was humid with an intermittent breeze from the river. I rang the bell. A few moments later, Mr. Stuhlmann answered the door, surprised to see a young, unknown woman gingerly holding a gift-wrapped package. When I explained my mission he graciously relieved me of the box, which he promised to give to Anaïs as soon as she returned from Europe. He told me that it was very lucky that I had found him home. He had planned to leave on a trip the day before, but had postponed his departure because of business. I, of course, attributed this serendipitous timing to fate and the validity of my goal. I felt I had done everything possible to reach Anaïs. Now I had to wait with the hope that she would respond.

In late June, the day before my twentieth birthday, about three months after my visit to Mr. Stuhlmann, I found a letter with a New York post mark waiting for me when I got home from school. It was from Anaïs, dated June 25, 1968, addressed to "Miss Beth," because I had signed my note to her using only my first and middle names, having experimented briefly with dropping my family name in a symbolic act of separation:

Dear Miss Beth: You must have been surprised not to hear from me. Many things prevented me from receiving your lovely gift — I returned to New York much later than I expected. Gunther Stuhlmann was in Europe. His assistant and I could not meet — she had the flu. Finally one day she took the package to her home and I called for it. What a surprise! Such a delicate gift - I love it — In October — the 23rd I will be lecturing at Berkeley University, Detroit, Michigan. Is that far from where you are? If it is not too far do let me know — Perhaps we can arrange to meet then. I will be back at 3 Washington Square Village in August — Do write me there. I am now leaving for a few weeks of rest — I had an over-burdened year, two books, one coming out in October (Novel of the Future) and Diary III in the Spring — besides a lecture a week. Are you a writer? It was thoughtful of you to write me — I prefer letters to reviews — they are more sincere. Thank you for your poetic and symbolic gift and for writing me.

Anaïs Nin

I read this letter from Anaïs like an answered prayer. Arriving as it did the day before my birthday, I interpreted it as a gift, an omen that our connection was destined. She had understood my longing and had answered it. She had recognized me. Now, perhaps, I could stand up to my parents' insistence that I remain under their roof and their control, narrow my hopes, dreams and plans to conform to theirs — marry, have children and live within a twenty minute drive from their front door. Now, perhaps, I could leave them.

Without hesitation, I wrote back to Anaïs informing her that Detroit was only a forty-five minute flight from Chicago and that I would be delighted to attend her lecture and meet her. I told my parents that I was doing a paper on the writer, Anaïs Nin, who would be giving a lecture in Detroit, and that it was too good an opportunity to miss seeing her in person. So it was arranged.

I remembered very little about the lecture itself, which was on *The Novel of the Future*, or about the audience, the weather, the flight. All I recalled was Anaïs's face and voice. At sixty-five, her delicate, ageless features set off her penetrating, inquisitive brown eyes. Wearing a long, flowing dress, her signature garb, adorned with silver jewelry, holding herself and moving like a dancer, she could have been a goddess in a myth, or a nyad in a fairy tale. When she laughed, the tip of her nose tilted slightly downward, giving her an expression of a delighted gamine. Her eyes were never completely still as she took in the audience, including everyone in her gaze. Perfectly harmonized with her appearance was her voice — soft but clear with the unmistakable reverberations of French and Spanish. Looking back, I realize that I was in a truly altered state in which time seemed to slow to a crawl yet flash forward at the speed of light. I wanted Anaïs to speak forever so I might memorize her cadences as reference points to my own thoughts, prolong the space-time continuum so the moment would never end.

But of course, it did. And Anaïs was immediately surrounded by autograph seekers with proffered books, well-wishers, and young women like me emboldened by their need to be close to her. I hovered at the outside of the circle, shy, hoping for a moment of privacy to introduce myself. But it was she who approached me. "You must be Margot. I knew I would recognize you." She told me that she was sorry that we would not have a chance to speak privately and asked me if I would continue to write to her.

Then she was whisked away to a faculty reception. I could not tell whether I was joyful because of her acknowledgment, or painfully disappointed by not having had a chance to speak more with her. When I got back home, I immediately wrote her a letter explaining that I had been happy to have met her and that I hoped one day to be able to spend more time with her. My letter to her crossed in the mail with her note to me:

Dear Margot: If I had known what you were like I would never have invited you to meet in a formal public way — I felt badly the moment I saw you. There are people created to meet alone and in quiet and in depth — Forgive me. Such dissonances between public and personal life always disturb me. I value the intimate far more — I should have guessed from your writing which is as fragile as the glass boat you gave me and almost evanescent. But do not disappear. Your face stood out from all the other faces, eloquent, and I gave you my friendship instantly —

I will be in New York until Nov. 26 — do write me.

Anaïs Nin

I did. And we began a correspondence and a relationship that lasted until her death in 1977. Because of Anaïs's
encouragement, I was able to leave Chicago. My parents made
sure to tell me they had turned my photographs to the wall
and said Kaddish, the mourners' prayer, for me. In spite of
being pronounced dead to my family, on January 1st, 1969,
I moved to Los Angeles to be close to Anaïs, who resided
there part-time with her husband, Rupert Pole. Though she traveled a great deal during the late 1960s and 1970s, when she
was home in Los Angeles, we would meet to discuss writing, the
challenges of being female in a patriarchal culture, the nature
of intimacy, politics, music, and art. I sometimes played viola
in the string quartet to which Rupert belonged, which met
at his and Anaïs's home on Friday nights. I supported myself
with various temporary jobs including being a fitting model,
waitressing, and clerical work.

Throughout the relatively short time we had together,
fate, serendipity, arbitrary events with personal meaning,
something was at play that added a sense of inevitability to our
relationship. One such event occurred when I fulfilled my
dream and moved to Paris in October of 1970. Through a
series of seemingly random connections, I wound up living at
18 Villa Seurat, the studio Anaïs had found for Henry Miller
in 1933. A friend of a friend knew of a studio for rent in
the 14th arrondissement, just when I had to relinquish my
temporary lodging. I had no idea when I moved into the
sunny loft near the Parc Montsouris that Anaïs had spent
many hours nearly forty years earlier in the place I now called
home. We only discovered this coincidence when I wrote
her with my new address and she quickly responded with

the revelation. Six degrees of separation had brought us full circle to what felt like another inevitable destination. We were both pleased to discover it, and at the same time it felt rather matter of fact. Our relationship had developed a quality of magical synchronicity that had begun to feel normal and not at all unexpected.

In the years after Anaïs's death, I not only became involved in psychology as a patient, but as a psychotherapist. In both contexts, I became increasingly interested in the ways in which early childhood experience informs development and also influences later relationships and decisions. I often thought of Anaïs and her belief in psychoanalysis, wondering about her experiences and wishing I had discussed the subject with her in greater detail when I had had the opportunity. Hoping her not-yet-published journals would answer my un-asked questions, I eagerly anticipated publication of each volume of her unedited diaries.

As the books were published, however, I finished reading each one with increasing distress and confusion, distraught to discover that the idealized maternal figure I had wanted and needed Anaïs to be, and whom she had presented herself to be, was not, in fact, who she was. After learning of her simultaneous marriages to Hugo Guiler in New York and Rupert Pole in Los Angeles, affairs with her analysts, and especially her affair with her father when she was an adult, I had great difficulty understanding how this woman who had always been so generative and forthright with me was at the same time leading a double life.

I had no way to understand how Anaïs could have told me that she believed the soul of the child she had miscarried had been reborn in me, to discover later that the "miscarriage" had been an abortion in the seventh month. Later, after meeting other young women who had also been close to Anaïs, I learned the declaration of progeny had been made to a number of them too. It was no less of a shock to discover that when Anaïs asked me if I might consider becoming Rupert's companion after her death, she was still married to Hugo Guiler and that several other women had received this same invitation.

Initially, I felt betrayed. The new information about Anaïs's life seemed to invalidate the relationship with the woman I had known and loved. I questioned the strength of our connection, my role in her life, my own need for her attention. If I had been a better friend, would she not have shared more of herself with me? Had I needed too much? Did she trust me? Over time, as I wrestled with these questions, I found myself flooded with sadness, knowing from my own experience, my psychological studies, and the histories of my own patients, that Anaïs must have suffered severe emotional trauma that precipitated such need to hide, to split her life into discrete compartments, and to engage in incest. I realized that I needed a new paradigm with which to understand this woman, who was both so dear to me and so alien.

In my efforts to orient myself and to integrate the new revelations about Anaïs's life, I re-read *Linotte*, the first volume of her childhood diaries, published in 1978, covering her life from eleven to seventeen years old. "Linotte," refers to the phrase "tête de linotte," a self-mocking reprimand that Anaïs employed and which translates approximately as "feather brain" in English. Reading *Linotte* again brought me back to

Anaïs as a little girl, traumatized by the loss of her father, her country, and her culture. She had no power in the world other than her own words with which to make meaning out of all that was happening to her. Re-reading *Linotte* allowed me to work backwards from the present to the past, picking up clues, evidence from the child about who the woman was to become. What had been opaque became more transparent, closing the chasm between true and false, fantasy and reality. Thinking about Anaïs with more of the facts of her life available, and with psychological theory and practice to structure my experience, I found that I could now understand her with much more compassion and clarity. As gaps in her history were filled in, a far more complex and multi-faceted woman emerged.

Personally and artistically Anaïs was a paradox. Accepting her as such and embracing her many contradictions seemed the most useful approach in providing a textured and comprehensive perspective from which to understand this woman who has been so deeply misunderstood by both her admirers and her detractors. Anaïs's childhood writings make her later life and work less remarkable for her relationships with famous men and women and the romantic and creative era in which she lived, than for her relentless courage to resolve the abuses of her childhood, integrate her many personae, and free herself to live a full and meaningful life.

Notes

1. Nin, A., 1967, p. 193

Part II

❧

A Brief Biography

What makes people despair is that they try to find a universal meaning to the whole of life, and then end up by saying it is absurd, illogical, empty of meaning. There is not one big, cosmic meaning for all, there is only the meaning we each give to our life, an individual meaning, an individual plot, like an individual novel, a book for each person. To seek a total unity is wrong. To give as much meaning to one's life as possible seems right to me.[1]

— Anaïs Nin

The Story of a Life[2]

1902: Cuba, April 11
An Ill-Fated Union

❧ Anaïs Nin descended from a family of propriety, scandal, poverty, and wealth. Her parents, Rosa Culmell and Joaquin Nin, were married in Cuba on April 11, 1902. Rosa was thirty years old and not yet married because, as the eldest of seven children, it was her duty to serve as surrogate mother to her four sisters and two brothers when their mother abandoned them in childhood. Rosa's mother, Anaïs, for whom Anaïs Nin was named, was of French and Cuban descent with a mind of her own. She ignominiously abandoned her husband and children to pursue a life of amorous adventure in Havana, eerily prefiguring her granddaughter's exploits. Rosa's father, Thorvald Christensen Culmell, was the Danish Consul to Cuba and a talented businessman whose import-export firm became a successful enterprise. By the turn of the century, he had amassed great wealth and social standing in spite of the shame brought upon the family by his unconventional and unfettered wife.

Joaquin Nin, Anaïs Nin's father, was twenty-two years old when he met Rosa. Born in Cuba, the son of a Spanish father and Cuban mother, he was baptized in Spain to avoid the stigma then attached to colonial birth. During this baptismal trip, the family decided to take up residence in Barcelona. When Joaquin was quite young, the family recognized his affinity for the piano and his gift for music. He studied composition and performance at the Barcelona Atheneum, gave his first public piano recital at age thirteen, and at age seventeen debuted as a soloist. Shortly after a well received solo recital at age nineteen, Joaquin abruptly sailed for Cuba. Speculations flourished as to the reason for the sudden departure of the popular young pianist. The two rumors that circulated with the most authority were that he had returned to Cuba to avoid military service in Spain or to flee the wrath of an angry father whose young daughter he had seduced.

Though Joaquin Nin was gifted, he was poor by Thorvald Christensen Culmell's standards, of questionable reputation, and of lower class than Rosa. Culmell did not approve of him. Rosa was infatuated. Despite the social embarrassment to her family she asserted herself, and insisted on marrying Joaquin against her father's judgment. But Señor Culmell's love and support for his eldest and favorite daughter were unwavering. As a wedding gift, he provided the couple with passage to Paris, an important European center for music, where Joaquin would teach and perform. He also gave him money to purchase a grand piano when the couple arrived, and a monthly income until Joaquin could earn enough to support himself and his wife, and begin a family.

1903: Neuilly, France, February 21ˢᵀ, 8:25 P.M. Under the Sign of Pisces

~ Almost exactly ten months after her parents' marriage, in the village of Neuilly-sur-Seine, a suburb of Paris, Anaïs Nin was born. Named after her maternal grandmother, her unusual name is associated with Athena, the Greek goddess of love, and with Anahita, goddess of the moon. Anaïs's aqueous birth sign, Pisces, became an important symbol to her throughout her life, and whenever possible, she preferred to live close to water.

1905 - 1907: St. Cloud, France
Sudden Illness, Dwindling
Finances, Dwindling Love

⌒ Shortly after her brother Thorvald's birth on March 12, 1905, when the family was in Cuba for a series of Joaquin's performances, the two-and-a-half-year-old Anaïs contracted typhoid fever. Her appearance changed almost overnight from a chubby, healthy toddler to a frail and sickly child. Her hair fell out and her bones protruded through her pale skin, giving her a skeletal appearance. Her father was horrified and repelled by her looks and made no secret of his disgust. He called his daughter "ugly," actively shunning her and avoiding physical contact.

Anaïs's mother, on the other hand, was frantic about her daughter's health. She hovered over the child, continually fearful that her daughter was at imminent risk of death. Nursing her sick daughter must have been all the more stressful as Rosa also had a new baby, as well as a pampered and demanding husband who insisted that his wife not only respond immediately to his every request, but that she be perpetually well groomed, coquettish, and ready to entertain friends and colleagues. Rosa and Joaquin began to bicker. The bickering eventually lead to quarreling, explosive hostility, and physical violence.

After Joaquin's performances in Havana, the family returned to France, this time accompanied by Rosa's sister, Juana. The official reason for Juana's presence was that she was unmarried, in her thirties, and father Thorvald was too ill to chaperon her social life in Cuba properly. The real reason for her presence, however, was to help Rosa and Joaquin with their finances. Because of father Thorvald's illness, Rosa's diminishing inheritance, and Joaquin's squandering of what money was available, the Nin coffers were low. The family moved from Neuilly to St. Cloud, to a smaller, less expensive house, and tried to economize by having Juana help with the children and contribute to family expenditures.

This arrangement turned out to be problematic. When Joaquin was away on tour, the household functioned smoothly and efficiently. When he returned to St. Cloud, however, he created strife and chaos, primarily with his sexual overtures toward Juana, which became a constant cause of hostility and bitter fighting between the sisters. Joaquin seemed to enjoy it.

As continued news of father Thorvald's declining health reached the sisters in St. Cloud, they strengthened their efforts to make peace between themselves. By the time of their father's death, the sisters had reconciled. In relative peace, the family went to Cuba to attend Thorvald's funeral. When they returned to St. Cloud, Juana did not accompany them.

1908: BERLIN, GERMANY
A VERY COLD WINTER

It was becoming evident that to gain financial security, Joaquin would have to win the support and admiration of the wealthy and flourishing German music establishment. Late in the summer of 1908, the family therefore moved to Berlin, Joaquin armed with honorary credentials bestowed by friends and colleagues. Rosa was in charge of the domestic well-being of her husband and two children, and was anticipating the birth of her third, to be named Joaquin Nin-Culmell. Shortly after his arrival, on September 5, 1908, his father left Berlin for eight months of touring in France, Germany, and Spain. Until late spring of 1909, Rosa was left alone to care for the three children and to survive a bitterly cold winter on a small allowance, and unable to speak German. Her husband meanwhile, enjoyed lavish accommodations, generous stipends, and an appreciative public.

1909 - 1913: Uccle, Belgium
A Family at War

⌒ Anaïs's sixth to tenth years were spent with her family in a large, rented house in Uccle, outside Brussels, Belgium, where Joaquin had been awarded a teaching position at the New University. By this time, her parents' anger towards each other had increased dramatically. The children were not only witnesses to violent scenes between Rosa and Joaquin, but were often victims of their father's beatings. "Here," Anaïs later wrote in her diary, "father's personality becomes more distinct."[3]

In this house the violence that marked Anaïs's childhood escalated and became a predictable horror of everyday life. Joaquin's efforts to impose his will on his wife soon grew into vicious beatings. When Joaquin learned that he could not subdue his willful spouse with physical force, he devised an even more diabolical method of punishing her. He beat her and locked her in the bedroom, then dragged the children to the attic and beat them, so their mother could hear their wails.

Also in Uccle, Joaquin, in a fit of temper and in full view of his children, brutally killed a neighbor's cat. His children suffered months of anxiety and nightmares.

During the family's tenure in Uccle, Joaquin also became obsessed with photographing his daughter in the nude. While muttering insults and critiques, adjusting lenses and light meters, insisting that Anaïs stand perfectly still and face him naked, Joaquin photographed his daughter again and again. She was never sure when her father would surprise her in her bath, as she dressed in the morning, or as she undressed at night.

In the meantime, she learned to speak French, a success that pleased her father, French being the preferred language of the aristocratic class in which he assumed membership. Otherwise, she spent her days helping her mother with the housework and looking after her brothers. She took piano lessons for a while, but demonstrated neither desire nor talent. She preferred to read, and spent many hours alone in her father's study, reading the novels on his shelves while he was away on tour. Her younger brother Joaquin had already displayed his father's talent for the piano and had begun lessons that he loved and to which he dedicated his energy and talent. Thorvald was withdrawn and practical. Though he showed a talent for the violin, he preferred mathematics, a choice that earned him his father's contempt.

In 1912, Anaïs faced a second life threatening illness. She had to have an emergency operation for a ruptured appendix. The surgery was complicated by a persistent abscess that had formed on the incision and which refused to heal. She remained in the hospital for nearly three months, making little progress toward recovery. When a second abscess formed in December, there seemed to be little hope. Joaquin was resigned to losing his daughter, though he became uncharacteristically involved with her during her illness, urging her to fight with all her strength to get well for his sake. Rosa refused to submit to what appeared to be an inevitable loss. She relinquished her fate to the care and wisdom of Sainte Thérèse de Lisieux, praying, fasting, and lighting candles. After a second operation was performed to clean and resuture the incision, amazingly, Anaïs recovered. She was well enough to leave the hospital in late winter, but was still quite weak, and her doctors recommended that she recuperate in a warmer climate. Therefore, on February 21, 1913, Anaïs's tenth birthday, the family moved to Arcachon, France, an Atlantic coastal village near the Spanish border.

Les Ruines, the house they rented in Arcachon, belonged to the wealthy Rodriguez family, friends from Cuba whom Joaquin had persuaded to become his patrons. The house was so named because it was built upon the partial ruins of a previous dwelling. Not only the ancient house was in ruins, however. The Nins' marriage was also in a state of disrepair that would soon lead to its demise.

The catalyst for the final break was Joaquin's involvement with the Rodriguezes's sixteen-year-old daughter, Maruca, who had become his student. Suspicious of Joaquin's attentions to the young woman, Rosa became increasingly jealous. Joaquin's physical abuse of his wife and children increased. He remained careful, however, in his relationship with Maruca, and her family. How much he was infatuated by her and how much by her father's money is not clear. Shortly after a confrontation between the two men, however, Joaquin left his wife and three children for good. Maruca subsequently became his mistress and then his wife of almost twenty years.

For months after her father left, Anaïs could not bear to be separated from her mother, and clung in desperation to the stuffed doll, Bouby, that her father had given her. She also became painfully shy and quiet, lost weight, spoke very little, and had difficulty sleeping. For a month, no one heard from Joaquin. Finally, he sent Rosa a terse note saying he had left for good, and advised her to move in with his parents in Barcelona.

The home of grandfather Joaquin Maria Nin Y Tudo and his wife, Angela Castellanos de Nin, was quiet and serene, primarily because grandfather's word was law and Angela obeyed him without question. Grandfather Joaquin was a retired military officer who had reared his son with beatings. Grandmother Angela was loving and affectionate. Anaïs quickly became attached to her. Rosa, who received no financial help from her husband, began giving voice lessons and performing to make ends meet. When Joaquin heard about this, he became furious and insisted that she stop. She would ruin his reputation. Much to Rosa's astonishment and affronted sense of justice, Joaquin's parents supported his wishes. When Rosa could no longer tolerate the brutal economic violence of her position, she secured a job teaching voice at the Granados Academy of Music and moved with the children to an apartment.

Anaïs, meanwhile, wrote poetry, stories, and a poignantly revealing play about a young girl and her blind father.[4] The father and daughter were very poor, but because he could not see, he was unaware of the squalid conditions in which they lived. To protect him from the truth, the girl made up stories when he asked her about their home, clothing, and surroundings. With words, the daughter embroidered fine fabric, polished wood, and grew spring flowers. When the father's sight was suddenly restored, the daughter was fearful he would be angry with her for lying, but the grateful father immediately understood the situation and appreciated his child's noble nature, loving her even more deeply for efforts to make his life beautiful.

In early summer, another of Rosa's sisters, Antolina, married and living in New York, convinced her to move the family to New York, too. There were more opportunities to teach music and perform, Rosa would be better able to provide for herself and the children, and Antolina could be of more help. Rosa and her sisters had lived in New York during the Spanish-American War in Cuba, spoke perfect English, and were at home in the culture of American life. Rosa agreed. Though there was no talk of divorce, the move to the United States was a bold symbolic statement of her intention to make a new life for herself and her family, as far away from Joaquin Nin as possible. The reason she gave to her children for the move was that their father was on an extended tour, and Rosa wanted to be closer to her sister.

1914 - 1920: On Board the Montserrat
The Diary Begins, New York, New Home

⌐ On July 25, 1914, in French, her language of choice until she was seventeen years old, Anaïs Nin, then eleven, made the first entry in the diary she would continue for the next fifty years:

Last look at Barcelona and last thoughts. The mountains rise up in majestic beauty. The setting sun shows its last pale rays. Here and there, the blue sky holds little white clouds. As I look at this landscape, my mind is crowded with thoughts. We are going to leave Barcelona, leave this beautiful country. No more shall I be able to touch my lips to the sweet face of dearest Grandmother. No more shall I be able to surrender to nameless thoughts that always come to me in the evening when I lean on the railing of our balcony, in the silence of the night. And last of all, I am sad to think that we are leaving a country that has been like a mother and a lucky charm for us.[5]

In August, the Nins moved to an apartment at 166 West 72nd Street that belonged to Antolina, who was in Cuba, where she maintained another home. Rosa industriously sought sources of income, from giving concerts and voice lesson to taking in mending and dressmaking. When she later bought a home of her own in New York, she rented out rooms to musician friends and family acquaintances. She also built up a business buying New York designer clothes for Cuban society women. She opened accounts at the best New York stores, charged the merchandise, and shipped the clothing to her Cuban clients, adding a 10% charge for her services. With the help of her sisters, and because of her reliability and good taste, Rosa had soon made a name for herself and her business quickly thrived.

While Thorvald and Joaquin adjusted to school and began making friends, Anaïs remained stubbornly aloof from her new culture. She cultivated a fierce allegiance to France and all things French. She chose to dress as a typical French school girl, in dark skirt, white sailor blouse, and white beret. Most of her classmates found her to be affected and standoffish.

She sought solace in the pages of her diary. It was her constant companion and dearest friend. Since beginning it en route to New York, she wrote in it faithfully. Obsessed with perfecting herself to be worthy of serving France, God, and her father, she recorded every compliment she received and made lists of sins and virtues in an attempt to improve her character. The list included failures such as anger, impatience, and vanity, and victories such as charity, sacrifice, and the recitation of evening prayers. Her subjects included family members and friends, the household tasks she performed, news of the war in Europe and her loyalty to France, and always, expressions of longing for her father. She copied into her journal every postcard and letter she received from him, and every response she mailed back, though she knew it disturbed her mother that she and her father corresponded. Her preoccupation with the hope of his return was a continuing theme:

January 3, 1915

... My thoughts can unroll and expand among these confidential pages. I am not discouraged because God didn't grant my wish [for her father to arrive on Christmas]. I am only more determined. I have renewed my vow, and if God is willing, Papa will be here on February 21, which is my twelfth birthday. I am full of hope. Why should God refuse to let me be with my Papa? Why should He refuse me this happiness that I have waited for all year? Since I realized that Papa wasn't coming, why did I begin to wish for his return? Alas, New York is far away, I am afraid that Papa won't be here the 21st of February either, that date that I have set my heart on.[6]

1915 - 1919: New York
Adolescence

The pages of the diary from Anaïs's twelfth through sixteenth years, are filled with descriptions of her daily life — her hardworking mother who was often demanding and critical of Anaïs, and whom Anaïs idealized, her dissatisfaction with school, her many flaws, reflections on the nature of familial interactions, and her correspondence with her father:

February 14, 1916

1. I study my heart. 2. I study life. 3. I study my lessons. 4. I study Joaquinito (who is really a strange little person). 5. Finally, I study the progress of sadness of which I am the victim (good or bad?).[7]

Anaïs also wrote about the war in her diary, and included fantasies of her wish to save France as Jeanne d'Arc had once done:

April 14, 1915

Oh, Joan, how I love you, how I admire you, oh, why did you have to leave this world! Look down upon the dangers to the glory of France, save her, protect her, oh, beautiful sweet heroine, and from heaven on high send us another heroine like yourself.... Oh, how I would love to be like her.[8]

She also confessed to a deep loneliness and isolation. Though expressed in dramatic and romantic language, these confessions describe Anaïs's efforts to combat the feelings of unlovability that plagued her:

November 23, 1916

Sometimes I feel as though I am forty years old because I think I have already suffered so much. I am ashamed of myself when I let myself dream of happiness, because I know, I understand that I deserve only misfortune, yet how much I have suffered and still suffer when evening comes. I have only one true friend left and that is my diary, which forces me to understand part of myself.[9]

August 17, 1917

You are my only friend right now, dear little diary...[10]

May 15, 1919

A single idea had taken possession of my dreams, a thing I had never, never thought of, an emptiness that I had never felt. I was alone and something was missing. It wasn't the love of my mother, my brothers or the rest of my family; I knew that I wanted someone very strong, very powerful, very handsome who would love me and whom I could love with all my heart. It is an image or an idol that my dreams have created and that I am searching for in mortal form. Does he exist? And there, under the starry sky, the moon, face to face with a horizon that doesn't go further than the end of the street, with my head in my hands, I sent a very sad prayer into infinite space: Love me, someone![11]

The year 1919, when Anaïs turned sixteen, was important for her in several ways. Maruca, her father's mistress, had been sixteen when Anaïs had last seen her, about six years earlier in Arcachon. We do not know for certain if Anaïs wondered about her own developing womanhood in relation to the object of her father's desire, but we do know she refused food and lost weight. She claimed that she was trying to help her mother economize, but her symptoms were much closer of those of anorexia nervosa, including the constant demand for self-perfection, the split between good and bad, and the conflict regarding her developing sexuality.

It was also in her sixteenth year that Anaïs recognized the tension between her need to be selfless and her conflicting desire to be the center of attention. In her diary, she set down the two sides of herself, referring to the "good" side as "Miss

Nin" and the "bad" side as the feather-brained "Linotte." It was Linotte who was thrilled by the way boys looked at her, who was obsessed with clothes, and who made dramatic hats that gave her an air of mystery. It was Miss Nin who could forego the purchase of fiction in favor of a practical cookbook on sale, who turned down invitations to dances and parties in order to stay home and help her mother, and who curtailed her own spending on clothing to conserve family finances. Linotte, Anaïs asserted, was her preferred personality, the one she valued most, but the one she felt she needed to hide in the privacy of her diary. The fact that she perceived herself as having two distinct personalities did not appear to disturb her, nor did it occur to her that these opposing selves could be integrated.

In April of Anaïs's sixteenth year, Rosa gave her daughter permission to quit her formal schooling. Having resisted formal education from the outset, Anaïs convinced her mother that because she had published several poems in the school newspaper, she was well on her way to becoming a professional writer, and could contribute to the family's finances that way. For the level-headed Rosa to accept this idealized fantasy made little sense. Still, she complied.

In early November of 1919, Anaïs received an especially strange letter from her father. After abandoning his family, Joaquin corresponded intermittently with Anaïs, indirectly relaying messages to Rosa through her, and causing tension between them every time a letter from him arrived. Correspondence from him was welcomed by Anaïs, but not unusual. What was out of the ordinary about this letter was the content. Normally, Joaquin wrote about his work, his travels, his successes, and his health. This letter, however, was full of innuendo regarding his relationship with Rosa and his insistence on his own honesty and irreproachable behavior as a husband and father. Anaïs showed her mother the letter, and asked her about it. Rosa, not one to mince words, explained to her daughter that her father had abandoned them all in Arcachon. Until that moment, Anaïs had believed that her mother had abandoned him, and taken her and her brothers away. Seemingly oblivious to her daughter's sensitivity about the loss of her father, or perhaps hoping the truth would free her daughter from her hopeless attachment to him, Rosa told Anaïs that her father, Joaquin, had been a cruel man who beat her and her children, that he never loved them, and that he was never coming to America. This reality was more than Anaïs could bear. She literally wept for days.

Shortly after this incident, Rosa had a nervous collapse. She was forty-seven. Whether or not the scene with Anaïs was a factor, the struggle of collecting rent from the boarders, giving voice lessons, and slow payment from her Cuban clients became too much for her to handle. Weeping, she took to her bed. During this time, Aunt Antolina took over, frightening the children with stories of their mother's impending death if things did not change.

Rosa soon decided the best plan to secure the family's future was to marry her daughter, who had developed into a beautiful young woman, to a wealthy Cuban businessman when she turned eighteen. Rosa's volatile sister, Anaïs Sanchez, had reluctantly agreed to sponsor her niece's society debut in Havana.

The same year, Anaïs became reacquainted with her cousin, Eduardo Sanchez, the youngest of Anaïs Sanchez's children. Eduardo was Anaïs's age. Though they had known each other all their lives, the handsome blond-haired, blue-eyed Harvard student became the object of Anaïs's most romantic fantasies, and soon became her closest confidant. Their relationship continued in various configurations, including a possible sexual interlude, throughout Anaïs's life. Both kept diaries, wrote poetry, and were considered by the family to be hopeless dreamers. One of their most important shared activities was the exchange of their diaries. Because of Eduardo's poor French, and Anaïs's inability to write in Spanish (which she had never formally learned), on June 9, 1920, when Anaïs was seventeen, she began writing her diary in English, the language she and Eduardo shared. This change in language represented an important emotional shift. Her insistence on writing in French had been an identification with her father, continuing the hope that he would return. Relinquishing French for English suggested, at least on a conscious level, that Anaïs was ready to make an attachment to someone in her current life. The closeness between Eduardo and Anaïs was not missed by their observant mothers. Eduardo's family was most concerned. He was expected to take his place in the family business and marry at an equal or higher social level.

Rosa realized that to ensure her daughter's future marriage to a wealthy man, she must respect her sister's wishes to keep the cousins apart. Therefore, she did not protest when, after Eduardo had returned to Cuba, his mother forbade him to have any contact with Anaïs. In defiance of his mother, he did manage to send a leather-bound journal to Anaïs as a declaration of his enduring love. In it he inscribed, "To my lost princess." [12]

The themes of lost love, impeded perfection, attachment, and incest became ever more evident in Anaïs's life. Her diary during this period was filled with romantic longing and the desperate need to be loved, overwritten in the elaborate prose of the 19th century romances that she so loved. It was also in Anaïs's seventeenth year that she began, "... consciously employing the technique of revision to refine the truth. In doing so, she was developing her style as a writer, which led to charges when the diaries were finally published that she rewrote the truth and therefore was a liar. In actuality, the matter was far more complicated, but it is safe to say that her obsession with refining the raw material of her life was so inhibiting that it interfered time and again with the creativity necessary for writing fiction."[13]

In her diary, Anaïs began to include more and more reflections about her goals and their inherent conflicts. Though she was well aware of the disappointments marriage could bring, she longed for love and the protection of a man. Yet she also had artistic ambitions and could not come to terms with how a woman could be both artist and wife. The most striking theme she entertained at this time, which became her guiding metaphor, was that her life would be "a dream made real."[14]

1921 - 1924: New York
Young Love, Early Marriage

⤳ Anaïs met Hugo Guiler in March of 1921. She was acquainted with his younger sister, who had invited Anaïs to a dance at their home. The young New York banker of Scottish descent had just graduated from Columbia University. He seemed to provide the magical bond Anaïs had longed for:

June 21, 1921

Do you know, it seems as if all the things I loved in Eduardo had come back to me in someone else, in an older person, and mixed with still more seriousness and wisdom. This is the impression I have of Mr. Guiler, that he knows, that he is strong, reliable, manly and yet with a poet's heart and mind. Oh, what may come of this stranger who has knocked at the door of my Inward World in the name of Poetry, Books? He has knocked, and I am thrilled, almost ready to open my door wide and exclaim: Welcome! Welcome![15]

Anaïs found Hugo to be the nearly perfect man: strong, patient, passionately interested in literature and the arts, handsome, and kind. He, too, kept a diary. Her dream of the ideal marriage was anchored in the image of her and her husband reading to each other from their diaries each night before retiring to each other's waiting arms. Her romantic idealism no doubt was encouraged by Hugo's admiration of her beauty, his suggestion that she was graceful enough to become a professional dancer, and his encouragement of her artistic ambitions.

Rosa was fond of Hugo, but found him an unsuitable match for her daughter because he was not Catholic. Hugo's family, of strict Protestant Scottish descent, was in a furor over their son's interest in a Spanish Catholic girl from a poor family. The family was further scandalized when Anaïs began working as an artist's character model, in other words, fully clothed, work her artistic European family found quite respectable. She was popular with many artists, including the illustrator Henry Dana Gibson, whose portrait of her graced the cover of the July 8, 1922 issue of "The Saturday Evening Post."[16] The additional income was necessary, because in June of 1921, Rosa, again overwhelmed by work, suffered a second breakdown.

One dynamic that stood out in Anaïs's modeling career was the contrast between her flirtatiousness and her outrage when she was propositioned. Anaïs's capacity for provocative sexuality and her concurrent denial may have stemmed from her need as a child to separate innocence and sexuality, when her father insisted on taking nude photographs of her. Her mother's attitude about sex certainly influenced Anaïs's, too. When, as a young woman of nineteen, Anaïs asked her to tell her about sex, Rosa responded that "it is like a man urinating, and not beautiful."[17]

In spite of everything, Anaïs and Hugo fell in love:

June 16, 1922

The young girl whose heart has been reflected here has ceased to be. She has passed from the state of conceiving to that of fulfillment, from wondering to that of deciding, from aspiring to that of choosing and making terms with life. All that has been was in preparation for the dawn of young womanhood to come — all that is to be, the story of its existence and consummation. Hands that knew only how to shape desires and aspirations, which were ever stretched to receive, now hold a man's happiness, are responsible for the molding of his destiny, and are stretched to give; to hold life's most precious gift; to comfort and sustain, and lift and to steer. This is no longer My Diary![18]

On June 6, 1922, Anaïs and Hugo became secretly engaged. Unaware of their son's betrothal, and desperate to separate him from her, Hugo's parents did what many upper class families did when such a crisis arose. They sent their son on the grand tour — three months travel in Europe. Hugo did not have the courage to disobey, and left for Europe on September 13, 1922. Assuming that her daughter had lost Hugo for good, Rosa arranged, with Antolina's financial help, for Anaïs to sail for Cuba in October of 1922 for the social season and the husband it would secure.

Though in her diary Anaïs described her departure for Cuba as a great sacrifice to save her family from ruin, she also enjoyed the appreciation she received from Cuban society. Her name was rarely missing from the society pages, which also included flattering photographs proclaiming her the belle of Cuban society. She pasted these clippings in her diary and sent others to Hugo in her daily correspondence with him.

Though Anaïs thrived on the Cuban upper-class social life, her heart was still devoted to Hugo. When he revealed plans

to join her in Cuba in February of 1923, she was relieved and
overjoyed, but also aware of conflicting feelings that she could
not easily quell. She was fearful of disappointing her mother,
who had gone to great trouble and expense to send her to Cuba
to find an appropriate husband. She also thought a great deal
about the sacrifices she might have to make in terms of her wish
to combine marriage and a career in writing:

July 4, 1922
    If to be wholly woman means to be an incomplete,
imperfect writer, well then I know which way to set my
course. I shall be Woman, in all its entity and perfection,
and succeed in that and the other will come of itself
and follow like a satellite and never be quite lost or
quite recovered or quite perfect, if you will, and yet
not quite dead either.

    And there you have it, whether it be true or false,
only time will say.[19]

On March 3, 1923, just twelve days after her twentieth
birthday, Anaïs Nin and Hugo Guiler were married in
a civil ceremony in Havana, with Aunt Antolina, Aunt
Juana, and several cousins present. The couple presented
their marriage to their families as a fait accompli. Their
families were not pleased.

1924 - 1928: PARIS
JOURNAL OF A WRITER AS A YOUNG WIFE

〜 Anaïs's journal entries during the first year of marriage presented an idyllic picture of a praise-worthy husband, a blissful wife, and an idealized portrait of their love and devotion to one another. Obvious by its absence, however, was sex. "The only indication of a problem may be found, more than a year after her marriage, in a reference to Hugo, 'whose delicacy and sensitiveness every day keep me from the things I had feared in life.' Her fear is of having sex." [20]

By December of 1924, Hugo had been promoted to the international division of his firm, which was located in Paris. He was already supporting himself, Anaïs, her mother and brothers. Rosa decided to bring Thorvald and Joaquin to Paris so Joaquin could study piano there.

For several months preceding the move, Anaïs also acted as long-distance negotiator between her parents, who were attempting to finalize their divorce. Her father was living in Paris and had served Rosa with divorce papers so he would be free to marry Maruca. Ironically, the stated reason for dissolution of the marriage was his accusation of Rosa's abandonment, which he was able to prove by her ten year residence in the United States. Enraged by his audacious lie, she fought for Anaïs's loyalty and exclusive support. So did Joaquin. During the final divorce proceedings, Anaïs confided to her diary that she felt much as she had when she was eleven. Loyalty to one parent meant disloyalty to the other. The shifting of allegiances and disillusionment with those she loved was one of the earliest themes of Anaïs's childhood. When imperfection colored an idealized relationship, Anaïs could not tolerate the disappointment and sought another perfect love.

Anaïs's move to Paris with Hugo and attendant kin, marked the beginning of her maturation as a woman and the beginning of her development as a writer. It was filled with hopeful anticipation and conflict, too. Paris represented a prestigious career move for Hugo, of which Anaïs was quite proud. The manner in which Hugo earned the money that supported Anaïs and her family, however, was becoming a source of disillusionment for her. Anaïs regarded Hugo's career in finance as inferior to her artistic life his income made possible.

Anaïs hated Paris when she and Hugo arrived in December of 1924. She found it dirty, and was intimidated by what she feared were the loose morals of the French and their interest in sensuality. Anxiety about her father's presence in Paris also contributed to her unease.

Her first year there, she experienced a recurrence of the symptoms she suffered upon her arrival in the States when she was eleven, including hypersomnia, lack of appetite, and sudden bouts of uncontrollable weeping. Though she did not seek him out, two days before Christmas, 1924, her father paid her a visit. He begged for her support in his continuing divorce proceedings. The meeting was difficult for Anaïs. She had not seen her father for ten years. In her diary, she reported she remained cool, objective and even agreed to dine with him and Maruca, now twenty-six years old. Her original intention had been to reject her father, enumerating his many crimes against her and the family, but she found she did not have the strength.

The initial meeting with her father and Maruca was indicative of many of the emotional, psychological confrontations she faced during her first four years in Paris. She was driven to meet head-on the things that she most feared, including sex, her role as wife and artist, her growing disappointment with Hugo, and the gaps in her education. She attempted, with varying degrees of success, to encounter the real world, while shaping it to avoid retraumatization and injury. There was also reason to believe that, in part, this frenetic push may have been a defense against depression.

Two important events occurred in 1925 that were catalysts for change in Anaïs's revulsion toward sex, and the gradual acceptance of her own desires. While she and Hugo were subletting an apartment at 15 Avenue Hoche from an American named Mr. Hansen, a business friend of Hugo's, Anaïs came across a stack of pornography. It introduced her to sado-masochism, prostitution, and erotic undergarments. She secretly read these illustrated tomes, and was both repelled and aroused by the graphic depictions.

The other erotic event of 1925 was the arrival in Paris of Hugo's instructor and father figure from Columbia University, the well-known author John Erskine. Because of Hugo's idealization of Erskine, Anaïs was determined to win him, to impress him with her intellect and beauty. She trembled with joy when he praised an essay she was working on about diary writing. What began as an idealized infatuation, however, later turned into a sexual obsession, and Anaïs's first real adventure into duplicity.

Erskine introduced Anaïs to his friend, Mme. Hélène Boussinescq, who encouraged her to enlarge her scope of intellectual interest and pursuit. Conversations with Boussie, as Mme. Boussinescq came to be called, helped Anaïs to overcome her bouts of depression, which Hugo referred to as "a kind of madness."[21] She and Boussie read and analyzed Edith Wharton, Madame de Stael, and others, unaware that Ezra Pound, James Joyce, Gertrude Stein, Ernest Hemingway, and many other contemporary writers were making literary history practically under her nose.

During her first four years in Paris, Anaïs also confided in her diary her conflict between her wishes to be a good, "selfless" wife and her impulse to be bad, meaning self-centered and imaginative:

May 29, 1926
How monstrously selfish I am with this big, noisy, voracious, passionate Self, turning wildly within its harmless-looking shell. Hugh, so good, so unselfish, works hard for our love. He is not to blame for not being a genius in art, for not having work to do at home so that our lives may flow together. When he is here, I am tamed. I am content to be his wife. His goodness makes me good. I crave no other companionship. My spirit rests. But he is seldom here. Oh, what a curse it is to be so much alive, so impatient, I who have so much, so perfect a love and home. What a curse it is to aspire forever to more and more when happiness is in my hands. I shall be punished.[22]

In the autumn of 1927, after a trip with Hugo to New York, where Anaïs enjoyed being much admired, her inhibitions loosened, and she began numerous exploits in multiple, contiguous sexual relationships. Hugo's substantial salary from National City Bank allowed him to provide his wife with bourgeois luxuries: personal hairdresser, maid, cook, and dressmaker. Trying to come to terms with the polarities she experienced between her ambitions to write and to be the perfect helpmeet, Anaïs focused her energies at this time on creating herself as the ideal banker's wife. She wore designer clothes and was no longer offended when, at business dinners and parties, Hugo's associates stared at her, captivated by her beauty, not listening to what she had to say. Her home became a masterpiece of design and decoration with every detail perfected.

With Hugo's encouragement, Anaïs began taking Spanish dance lessons and started performing professionally. One afternoon, after her weekly lesson, her instructor, Señor Paco Miralles, followed her into the dressing room, bent to his knees and, while she was still dressed, kissed her between her legs. Though nothing more came of this overture, it sparked the internal war between what she called her "Catholic prudishness" and her "Latin sensuality."[23]

It was then she began a diary within the diary, called "Imagy."[24] Like the split between Miss Nin and Linotte, this diary within the diary also demonstrated Anaïs's difficulty, or inability, to recognize and integrate conflicted desires or wishes. In Imagy, Anaïs recorded Miralles's passionate gazes, her desire to see Eduardo and Erskine, who were in the States, and her wish that she could accept Hugo and their love could be enough to make her happy.

Still sexually awkward, she and Hugo had openly begun to

discuss sex and to experiment. They obtained a copy of the *Kamasutra*. In euphemistic prose, Anaïs described the loving arts in which they blissfully communed. Perhaps because of the couple's greater intimacy, Hugo, then thirty, broached the subject of children with his twenty-four-year-old wife:

> Her excuses were numerous: they are lovers, not responsible parents; she is too busy with dancing; and she still does not feel free from her own mother. She is also too easily fatigued. Perhaps the most important excuse is that she is determined to remain what she calls "the Other Woman." She will not be abandoned like her mother, but one of the women her father always sought (later she will use the word "mistress"). Certainly she is not ready for motherhood, for she is still split into two women: one pure and loyal, the other (whom she describes in far greater detail) impure and restless.[25]

At the end of April, 1928, Hugo's father died, just ten days before he was to make his first visit to see his son and daughter-in-law in Paris. Hugo was inconsolable. The image of his suffering strengthened Anaïs's resolve never to be the cause of any pain to him. Hugo and Anaïs sailed to New York to be with his family, but Anaïs escaped for a few hours each day to meet with friends and family members. One luncheon meeting in Manhattan was with Eduardo. Much to her shock, he informed her that he was homosexual and had entered psychoanalysis in an effort to be cured. This revelation was Anaïs's first encounter with both homosexuality and psychoanalysis. She confided to her diary her guilty concern that if she had pursued a sexual relationship with her cousin, perhaps he would not have developed a sexual response to other men.

Hugo and Anaïs returned to Paris at the end of May, 1928. That October, when Anaïs was twenty-five years old, John Erskine moved to Paris with his wife Pauline and their two children. Anaïs was still intimidated by her husband's beloved mentor, but was determined to win his respect and interest. When Pauline confided to Anaïs that Erskine had complained of being restless and wanting more romance, Anaïs accepted the confidence as a way to get closer to him. When the couples were together, dining or having drinks, Anaïs emphasized the importance of the physical in love relationships. Erskine assumed she was a woman of amorous experience, and soon he confided to her that he was in love with an American woman, Lilith, who would soon be visiting him in Paris. Anaïs offered to lie for him if he needed an excuse to be alone with his mistress.

1929: Paris
The First Infidelities

The following February, just before he was to leave for New York, Erskine visited Anaïs with his mistress, Lilith. Though Anaïs was pleased to take on the special role of Erskine's confidante, she confessed to her diary her sympathy for Pauline and the children. Erskine returned to Paris and his family by the middle of April and made plans with Hugo and Anaïs to vacation with them in Burgundy. During the vacation, Anaïs and Erskine confessed their mutual attraction.

In May, the morning after a formal dinner the Erskines and Guilers attended together, Erskine appeared at Anaïs's door while Hugo was at work. They kissed and caressed one another, with Anaïs dressed only in a Spanish shawl. They attempted intercourse, but Erskine was not able to penetrate her. Shortly thereafter, the Erskines returned to the States. Anaïs found herself in a vortex of agitated longing she attempted to soothe in part by submerging herself in a flurry of writing. It included a series of short stories called *Waste of Timelessness*.

The stock market crash on Black Friday in November of 1929 brought financial and emotional strain to Hugo and his extended family, as it did to the rest of the world. His persistent worries about money and finance began to spawn quarrels between him and Anaïs. His financial concerns also broke through her denial that Hugo was a banker, a businessman, and possibly would never be an artist. In her diary, she confided her despair at the discovery of her husband's lack of imagination and creativity.

1930 - 1931: PARIS
FANTASIES OF FULFILLMENT

In December of 1929, two months before her twenty-seventh birthday, Anaïs read D.H. Lawrence's novel, *Women in Love*. Captivated by his evocation of women's capacity for passionate emotional and sexual connection, she found herself critical of, and disappointed with, Hugo's compliance with her, the ease with which she was able to influence him. During this period, Anaïs coined the term "mensonge vital," or "necessary lie"[26] to describe the fabrications she later employed to protect Hugo from her infidelities.

Her goal of achieving balance between artistic creation and a satisfying relationship remained agitating. In the winter and spring of 1930 she was increasingly restless, depressed, and anxious. She worried that she had heart trouble. She threw herself into her dancing, rehearsing obsessively, performing as often as possible. She also ate very little, surviving mostly on liver extract, coffee, and sedatives. When she finally agreed to see a doctor, she was diagnosed with pernicious anemia and depression.

The death of D.H. Lawrence in the spring of 1930 came as a painful shock to Anaïs. She had planned to write to him to begin a correspondence. Instead, she determined to write an essay about his work, hoping to bring him posthumously the appreciation she felt he had not properly received. For financial reasons, that summer, Anaïs and Hugo left the spacious Paris apartment where they had lived with Rosa and Joaquin (Thorvald had gone off on his own by this time) and moved to a large, but reasonably priced house in the village of Louveciennes, a small town about half an hour west of Paris by train.

Meanwhile, Eduardo Sanchez also moved to Paris, hoping to be "healed" from homosexuality via psychoanalysis. He and Anaïs began spending a great deal of time together, discussing Lawrence, modern literature, and especially psychoanalysis. She insisted that her diary was her analysis.

In October, her essay, "D.H. Lawrence, Mystic of Sex," was published under the pseudonym Melisendra, by *The Canadian Forum: A Monthly Journal of Literature and Public Affairs*. In a burst of pride, she sent a copy to John Erskine, who praised the work and encouraged her to begin using her own name in her submissions. Though she completed a great deal of fiction during the fall and winter, her stories were returned unread by Janet Flanner of *The New Yorker*, and Sylvia Beach at *Shakespeare and Company*, H.L. Mencken, at *American Mercury*, did not respond at all.

As well as focusing a great deal of energy on her writing and flirtations with two literary editors, during the fall of 1930 and winter of 1931, Anaïs also committed much creative effort, with Eduardo's help, to decorating what became the metaphor for her experience of her compartmentalized self — the house at Louveciennes. Djuna, Anaïs's protagonist from *Children of the Albatross*, described a fictionalized Louveciennes:

> Then the image of the house with all its windows lighted — all but one — she saw as the image of the self, of the being divided into many cells. Action taking place in one room, now in another, was the replica of experience taking place in one part of the being, now in another.
>
> The room of the heart in Chinese lacquer red, the room of the mind in pale green or the brown of philosophy, the room of the body in shell rose, the attic of memory with closets full of the musk of the past.[27]

Though she spent a great deal of energy on her creation of Louveciennes, Anaïs also made time to write, which paid off in another publishing victory in early 1931 — the acceptance of her full length manuscript on Lawrence, *D.H. Lawrence: An Unprofessional Study*. Elated at her success, she was beginning to feel much more at home in the cultural life of Paris, but less at home in her own psyche.

That spring, she undertook more serious psychoanalytic readings, including further works of Freud, Jung, and Adler. Her own behavior caused her more dilemmas, however. During another trip to New York with Hugo, she spontaneously lied to Erskine, with whom she was still obsessed and who was currently in the process of leaving both his wife and mistress. She told him that she was having an affair with Aldous Huxley, whom, in fact, she had never met. The lie made Erskine jealous and more attentive. "Anaïs secretly laughs at Erskine and concludes that most people like to be lied to, for a lie 'heightens' life."[28]

Hugo, who was exquisitely sensitive to Anaïs's moods, finally questioned her on the nature of her relationship with Erskine. Eventually, she confessed the whole story and invited Hugo to read the diary pages recording Erskine's failed attempt to have intercourse with her. Hugo was devastated, whereas Anaïs was relieved finally to have exposed the truth. The couple fought for weeks, each quarrel followed by intense and passionate sex. Hugo needed to forgive Anaïs, to believe in her purity in order to continue to believe in his marriage. Of his wife's dalliance with Erskine he wrote, "And so my pity reasserted itself again over my pain, for I realize that she has suffered even more than I have."[29]

On November 30, 1931, Anaïs and Hugo dined with Hugo's attorney friend John Osborn. Osborn enthusiastically reported that his good friend from the States, Henry Miller, would like to accompany him to Louveciennes for lunch, to meet Anaïs, the woman who had written so eloquently about

Lawrence. The meeting of Anaïs Nin and Henry Miller on December 5, 1931, altered both their lives, personally and professionally, forever.

The rough-spoken, forty year-old American from Brooklyn regaled Anaïs with stories of debauchery, of prostitution, and of his sociopathic and exquisitely beautiful wife, June, for whom he had left his first wife and child. The soft spoken and alluring twenty-eight year-old Anaïs was Henry's dream of the ideal woman.

Anaïs and Henry spent many hours together in long conversations about writing, shared their diaries and manuscripts in progress, and discussed Henry's most pressing problem, his mistrustful and volatile relationship with June. Several weeks later, when June arrived in Paris, Henry brought her to Louveciennes to meet Anaïs. Anaïs found June's blonde beauty to be the perfect complement to her own, and she became immediately obsessed with her. June's stories of her affairs with other men and women were evidence to Anaïs of June's independence and strength, her open quarreling with Henry during dinner a banner of emotional reality. She felt that she and June were each other's mirrored selves.

1932: PARIS
PASSION FULFILLED

After June returned to New York and Henry left for Dijon to take a job Hugo had found for him, teaching English in a boys' boarding school, Anaïs became increasingly depressed and anxious. She wrote volumes of letters to Henry, which he answered immediately, and an equal number of epistles to June, to which she received no response at all. To calm her nerves, she spent several weeks at a spa in Switzerland, taking the waters, having massages, and altering the slight downward slope of her nose with cosmetic surgery.

When she returned to Louveciennes in February of 1932, just before her twenty-ninth birthday, it was with new determination to take on her role as dutiful wife. Shortly after, Henry returned from Dijon, began working for the Paris edition of the *Chicago Tribune*, and meeting Anaïs daily in the cafés of Montparnasse. Toward the end of February, 1932, Anaïs again became overwhelmed by her need for physical passion. She started using the apartment of her friend, Princess Natasha Troubetskoi, as a private address to exchange love letters with Henry.

Soon, Anaïs found herself in a state of anxious arousal. Still fearful of actually committing adultery, she spent days with Henry skirting around the subject of their growing attraction for one another, the physical contact she both feared and longed for. On March 2, 1932, shortly after her twenty-ninth birthday, Anaïs wrote to Henry, "I will be the one woman you will never have"...[30] Six days later, in a cheap hotel room, Henry and Anaïs consummated their passion.

Four days after her first sexual interlude with Henry, Anaïs took Hugo to a brothel that Henry had told her about where the prostitutes performed exhibitions of sexual techniques and where the patrons could participate if they so chose. During one exhibition, in which Anaïs and Hugo decided not to participate, Anaïs first discovered the existence of the clitoris, "... a new place in the woman's body, the source of a new joy which I had sensed sometimes but never definitely." [31]

She described the evening at the brothel as a tremendous success. She soon faced a problem regarding her lover, however. Hugo found Anaïs's diary and discovered her infidelity:

> ... she persuaded him — because of course he wanted to be persuaded — that this was an "imaginary" journal "of a possessed woman" and not the "real one." The "real one," she insisted, was just like the red in size and shape but it had a green cover. She had temporarily misplaced it, but would find it and show it to him when he returned from the bank that night. She then rushed to the little shop in Paris where she bought all her diaries in those years, and worked at double speed and in deep secrecy to write enough entries to bring the green journal up to date with the red. And so she convinced Hugo that the red (which was really "true") was "false," and the green "decoy diary" (which was really "false") was true.[32]

In March of 1932, Henry moved to Clichy, a northern working-class suburb of Paris. Anaïs promised she would support him, secretly giving him half of the money Hugo gave her for household expenses. The two-and-a-half years Henry lived in Clichy were one of the most creative periods of both his life and Anaïs's. Their sexual and personal relationship deepened and developed, informing their writing. Conversely, their artistic productivity influenced and enhanced their personal relationship. In her journal, Anaïs faithfully recorded the details of their discussions about literature, psychoanalysis, film, music, travel, philosophy, and food, as well as their many sexual explorations and discoveries — details she edited out of the originally published diaries of this epoch.

Henry, unlike Hugo, did not offer unconditional praise for Anaïs's writing. Though his criticisms were difficult for Anaïs to accept, her writing greatly benefitted from them. Henry insisted on taking her work seriously, going over it carefully. He was moved by the quality of her writing, by her perceptions, analyzes, and ideas. He urged her to make use of her diary as a source for fiction. Anaïs complained to Henry she felt awkward and blocked writing a third-person narrative, but when she switched to first person, present tense, the writing came easily.

Because of her creative block, Eduardo convinced Anaïs to try psychoanalysis. He had recently begun treatment with René Allendy, one of the original twelve founders of the Psychoanalytic Society of Paris and a member of the first generation of psychoanalysts. Allendy drew Anaïs's interest because of his theories about the artist's use of dreams and the need to resolve neuroses to free the artist to live in the world and create without impediment.

It is important to note that in the early days of psychoanalysis, patriarchy was even more entrenched than it is today. Post-Victorian assumptions that women were intellectually, morally, and creatively inferior to men were discussed by Freud, particularly in his writings about the Oedipus complex, superego development, and the origins of hysteria. His initial theory about hysteria proposed that sexual abuse was its cause. Under pressure from the psychoanalytic community, however, he later repudiated this theory, replacing it with the hypothesis that a child's unconscious wish to seduce the parent of the opposite sex, not actual abuse, was at the core of hysterical symptoms. Only later were other influences recognized as critically important, including mysogenistic cultural norms, interpersonal dynamics, and the undeniable reality of child sexual abuse. The primary focus of early psychoanalysts, including Allendy, was on adult sexuality and aggression.

Anaïs began psychoanalysis with Allendy on April 22, 1932. She recorded their sessions in her diary and, as might also be expected, they focused on her relationships with men. She was flattered when Allendy told her she was the most important woman in Eduardo's life. He explained to her that it was possible the only cure for Eduardo's homosexuality might be for her to have an ongoing sexual relationship with him. Anaïs insisted that her love for Eduardo was familial and declined to take responsibility for curing him. Though she felt Allendy was correct that her father's abandonment had caused her great trauma, she did not agree with his interpretation that her cultivation of dramatic flair and ethereal charm was the result of having witnessed her parents engage in sex when she was a child. In keeping with the theories of the time, Allendy also told Anaïs her seductive manner was the result of her wish to seduce her father, rather than the result of having been seduced or abused by him. During one session in which Anaïs and Allendy were discussing her concerns about not having a full bosom, she unbuttoned her blouse and showed him her bare breasts. She was gratified by his admiration and recorded every word in her diary. Eroticism had entered another relationship.

As the summer of 1932 drew to a close, Anaïs's emotional life became more and more complex. Wanting to win Henry's exclusive devotion (he upset her by confessing that he sometimes visited prostitutes), she attempted to make him jealous of Allendy, Hugo, and Erskine, too. As her feelings of competition, jealousy, and insecurity continued to grow, Anaïs fought back by attempting to provoke her admirers and thus assert her power over them. To Allendy, she exaggerated Henry's thoughtlessness. To Henry, she alluded to the erotic undertones of her meetings with Allendy. And with Eduardo at a club one evening, she openly flirted with another young man. Then she invited Henry to dine with her and Hugo and spend the night in the guest room at Louveciennes.

Further complicating the deceptions, Anaïs urged Hugo to begin psychoanalysis with Allendy. Why Allendy agreed is a question that remains unanswered. To analyze husband, wife, and cousin, while maintaining a growing erotic relationship with the wife, certainly violated norms of practice, even in the early days of psychoanalysis. To Anaïs, though, the incestuous nature of these overlapping relationships was very similar in structure to her early family dynamics:

Now she is feeling like a "most corrupt" woman with a Madonna face. "I will practice the most incestuous crimes with a sacred religious fervor.... I will swallow God and sperm." Then she lists the following sins in her diary: love for her own blood (Eduardo), her husband's spiritual father (Erskine), a woman (June), the woman's husband (Henry), and her analyst (Allendy), who is Eduardo's spiritual father and now Hugo's guide. And all her sins are committed beautifully, she adds. Now she has fully embraced the bad girl created by her father's abuse.[33]

Then June returned to Paris. Once again, Anaïs experienced herself to be merging with June in a fusion of erotic attraction and maternal devotion, likely propelled to some degree by the guilt she felt by her betrayal of June with Henry. The two women were engaged in a competition to win Henry's devotion, yet focused most of their attention and time on each other, more or less ignoring Henry in the process. The underlying fault lines in this triangulated relationship rendered it more and more unstable. One drunken night, it erupted into a violent confrontation between Henry and June. The truth about his relationship with Anaïs, was exposed. There could be no return to any pretense of innocence. June threatened Henry with violence. Anaïs gave him the fare to go to London for Christmas, to get him away from Paris while June was still there. Just before he left, however, June accosted him and demanded all his money. He complied. A friend managed to scrape together the fare for him, but because he arrived in England without a penny, the police sent him back to France, worried that he was indigent and would end up on the dole. He immediately went to Louveciennes where he and Anaïs spent a blissful ten days alone together. Hugo was away on business, and June had finally gone.

1933: PARIS
MULTIPLE RELATIONSHIPS, FIDELITY TO WRITING

To please Allendy, Anaïs told him she had followed his advice and broken off sexual relations with Henry. Perhaps because he believed her so easily, he began to fall in her esteem. He no longer appeared to her to be quite the powerful presence she had first idealized. She was also becoming fascinated by another analyst, Otto Rank, whose 1932 publication of *Art and Artist* she and Henry had read. Anaïs remained interested in Allendy though, at least in part because of his affiliation with and financial support of the French surrealist artists, the most notable being Antonin Artaud. The primary tenets of the surrealist movement were ones with which Anaïs strongly identified, including the importance of the dream to the creative process and the necessity of free imagination and spontaneity.

At Anaïs's urging, Allendy introduced her to Artaud. He soon suspected an attraction between them, became jealous, and warned Anaïs that Artaud was a drug addict, mentally ill, unstable, and, furthermore, homosexual.

Allendy also attempted to assert his importance in her life by convincing her to accompany him to a hotel, where they consummated their sexual relationship. Anaïs reported to her diary that she was terribly disappointed with Allendy's flabby body, lack of sexual finesse, and general awkwardness.

The most important object of Anaïs's attentions in the spring of 1933 was not Hugo, Henry, Eduardo, Allendy, or Artaud. It was her father. Since acting as go-between almost ten years earlier during her parents' divorce, she had barely spoken to him. Suddenly, on a May afternoon, Joaquin Nin telephoned Anaïs at Louveciennes to say he was on his way to see her. Hugo was at work, Henry had just been fed and sent back to Clichy, but Artaud was meeting her for dinner. Anaïs hurriedly sent a telegram to him, canceling their plans. She was free to see her father.

The reunion was a dramatic enactment of reconciliation.

They welcomed one another with the relief and intensity of two lovers parted by fate, who could now rejoice in their mutual rediscovery. Joaquin Nin found in his beautiful daughter the perfect female reflection of himself. He invited her to join him and Maruca at the Riviera, joking with pleasure that when he introduced Anaïs to his friends as his daughter, they would assume that she was his mistress:

> ... she fills her diary with description and analysis of him and their discussions of their "twinship": their petite builds, similar height, thin lips, tapered hands, fragility, artistic temperament, indifference to food. Both love music, the sea, sobriety, and have a great need for cleanliness and order (he to the point of washing his hands every ten minutes, a repetition compulsion disorder). They have a passion for aesthetics, creation and drama (both wear capes), and both achieve their desires through deception... They have pride and strong wills, and each suffers, she concludes, "from romanticism, quixotism, cynicism, naïveté, cruelty, schizophrenia, multiplicity of selves, dédoublement, and each is bewildered as to how to make a synthesis." They pour their genius into living — their only indulgence is lovemaking — and their talent into their art. [34]

Against Hugo's advice, Anaïs agreed to accept her father's invitation to meet him and Maruca later in the summer for a seaside vacation. In the meantime, keeping Hugo, Henry, Allendy, and Artaud happy had begun to take a toll on her. Artaud finally accused her of toying with Allendy, intentionally hurting him, and being fickle. Wanting to resolve the growing tension between them, Anaïs felt she and Artaud should begin a sexual relationship. Dressed in a costume of red, silver, and black, Anaïs arrived at his door unannounced. They aroused each other with aggressive foreplay, but Artaud could not maintain an erection with her. Their relationship became further strained because of Artaud's loyalty to Allendy. His early idealization of Anaïs devolved into hostility and near paranoia. The relationship attenuated and finally dissolved.

In the meantime, the shadow of incest that darkened Anaïs's early childhood was about to become a reality. Anaïs anticipated her trip to visit her father and Maruca in the south of France as a respite from her chaotic relationships. As it turned out, Joaquin Nin was not accompanied by his wife when he arrived at his hotel in Valescure-St. Raphael. Soon, the flirtations and posing between him and Anaïs that began at Louveciennes earlier in the year continued at the hotel, each confiding stories of conquests and dissatisfactions with present lovers. One night, as the two were talking — Joaquin lying in bed, Anaïs sitting at his side — he asked her to kiss him. She did. Anaïs and her father became lovers during the last week of June, 1933. Anaïs wrote in her diary that she believed she had found the perfect love for which she had been searching.

During the summer of 1933, with her incestuous relationship consigned to the pages of her diary, Anaïs continued to work on the manuscript that became *House of Incest*. The incestuous affair, however strangely it began, evolved in a most ordinary way. Anaïs's idealization of her father was being tried. Back in Paris, she had become a frequent visitor to the apartment where he lived with Maruca, but had begun to tire of his constant requests of her, his criticism of her artistic life, particularly of Henry, and his contempt for modern writers. She was disappointed that her father, with whom she so identified and who claimed to understand and appreciate her as an artist, could treat her as he did everyone else in his life — as an extension of himself, available to meet his every need.

Unable to accept Allendy's interpretations and advice on the subject, once she finally confided in him, Anaïs searched for help and answers elsewhere. After reading all of Rank's work, she dared again hope that it would be he who might understand and help her. On November 7, 1933, she consulted him for the first time. Anaïs and Rank explored her past, her conflicts and relationships, and, most importantly to Anaïs, her artistic goals. He observed that the source of Anaïs's many selves came from the discomfort she experienced between her ideal self and her actual self. Creating many personae was a way of influencing her own self-criticism and controlling the approving responses of others. He believed that the diary had come to function in a similar way. She could not freely create fiction because she was so intent on presenting a flattering image of herself on the diary's pages. Her analysis with Rank lasted five months, from November, 1933 until March of 1934.

She felt that Rank helped her to live and create in the real world. She also began a new work, which would later be published as *Winter of Artifice*, a novella about her father. Because of her work with Rank, she also became more objective about her father's increasing demands on her. Any difference between them he experienced as a betrayal or criticism of him. He was offended if Anaïs chose a different brand of cigarette to smoke, or preferred a different composer or writer. She began to realize that his interest in her was as his mirror image, not as herself. When he told her of his planned seduction of a young violinist, she confronted him with his cruelty and his manipulation of her feelings and those of his prey. He retaliated with accusations and details of his disappointments with her. Six months after their incestuous relationship began, it came to a contentious end.

Anaïs was now able to be more truthful with herself, if not with others. She recognized she was deeply dissatisfied in her marriage with Hugo, though she was still unable to leave him because of her financial dependence. Probably sensing that his wife was feeling emotionally more distant from him, and wishing to be closer to her, even by proxy, in the spring of 1934 Hugo began analysis with Rank.

1934: Paris
Psychoanalysis, Pregnancy, Abortion

In spring of 1934, Anaïs discovered that she was pregnant. Because she had once been diagnosed by a gynecologist as infertile, she did not consider pregnancy a possibility, denied the obvious symptoms, including morning sickness, and did not seek professional help for months. On May 16th, she finally visited a doctor, who confirmed her suspicions. Though Anaïs was sure Henry was the father, it was crucial to her that Hugo believe the child was his. (She apparently never considered that her father might be the father of her child). To prepare the way for disclosing her pregnancy to Hugo, she rekindled their sex life in a campaign to win his trust and allay his suspicions. When she revealed to him that she was pregnant, he was delighted.

It is not clear if Anaïs ever planned to carry the child to term. Her diary indicates mostly conflict and guilt. Henry did not want to father another child, and Anaïs felt guilty about deceiving Hugo. She also believed that having a child would disable her as a writer and lover. "I must destroy it ... it is a choice between the child and Henry, she asserts. He does not want it. I can't give Hugh a child of Henry's. Furthermore, motherhood ... is an abnegation ... the supreme immolation of the ego." [35]

Keeping her plans secret from Hugo and her mother, Anaïs found a sage-femme, or midwife, who promised she could provide her with appropriate potions and elixirs to induce a miscarriage. In the meantime, feeling more confident and sure of her future, Anaïs decided that it was time for her to begin a sexual liaison with Rank. He had confided to her that he was terribly unhappy in his marriage. On June first, 1934, in his office, Rank and the pregnant Anaïs began a sexual relationship. The good father figure of Rank replaced the bad father of Joaquin Nin.

Yet, Anaïs was also still devoted to Henry, who was unaware of the nature of her relationship with Rank. She traveled from an assignation with Rank to a tryst with Henry with ease and confidence. She felt full of energy, power, control, and passion. When a small studio at 18 Villa Seurat became available, Anaïs decided it would be the perfect place for Henry to live for the rest of the summer. She had provided Henry with two other important gifts that summer — the money to underwrite the publication of his *Tropic of Cancer* and an eloquent preface to the book.

By the end of August, the ministrations of the midwife had not yet produced results. Anaïs finally agreed to see a doctor, a friend of Rank's who confirmed she was still pregnant, in fact, almost seven months pregnant. In desperation, she decided to have an abortion, which had to appear to be a miscarriage. She met with the doctor in an empty apartment where he began the procedure that took a week to come to completion:

August 29, 1934

I sat in the studio, talking to my child ... It would be better to die, my child, unborn; it would be better to die than to be abandoned, for you would spend your life haunting the world for this lost father, this fragment of your body and soul, this lost fragment of your very self. There is no father on earth. The father is this shadow of God the Father cast on the world, a shadow larger than man .... It would be better if you died inside of me, quietly, in the warmth and in the darkness.[36]

The work of the abortionist was successful. Several days after a saline solution was introduced into her uterus, Anaïs began to bleed. In a panic, Hugo — who assumed she was having a miscarriage — rushed her to the hospital. Eduardo, who was living at Louveciennes, accompanied him. Rank hurriedly returned from London where he was giving a lecture. Her cousin, her analyst, a remorseful Henry, who believed the child was his, and a tortured Hugo, who believed he had fathered the child, were all in attendance. In *Incest*, the unexpurgated diary of this time, Anaïs recounted how, in the midst of the excruciatingly painful delivery of her dead infant girl, she carefully made herself up to look her best for her four men and the doctors and nurses attending her.

In the expurgated first-published volume of Anaïs's diary, she presented the incident as a late-term miscarriage. It is one of the most moving and well-known passages in all of her work. She also recreated the event in fiction, ending *Winter of Artifice* with this description:

> The last time she had come out of the ether it was to look at her dead child, a little girl with long eyelashes and slender hands. She was dead. The little girl in her was dead too. The woman saved. And with the little girl died the need of a father.[37]

The events of the fall, including the abortion, exhausted and depleted Anaïs. She felt less tolerant of Henry's seeming disregard for money—his assumption that she could always get more (from Hugo) to pay his bills, including sponsoring *Tropic of Cancer*. The complexity of her life again became draining and unmanageable. As Rank was preparing to depart for New York, Henry was basking in satisfaction with his anticipated publication, Hugo was frustrated and anxious over recent financial setbacks and the loss of Anaïs's child. Anaïs, distraught and feeling marginalized, began brief liaisons with two of Hugo's friends.

In late November of 1934, as planned, Anaïs sailed for New York to study with, or more accurately, to be with Rank, who had been sending her letters of loving devotion all fall. Believing she was finally tiring of the demanding Henry, Hugo happily gave his blessing for her to go study psychoanalysis. He planned to meet her in New York in January. Henry believed she was traveling to the States with Hugo and that she intended to study with Rank so Henry could join her and the two of them could open a psychoanalytic practice together. Rank believed Anaïs had abandoned Henry and Hugo, as well as the idea of becoming an analyst, and was planning to live with him.

When Anaïs arrived in New York, Rank was at the dock to greet her, and they commenced a glorious social life among Rank's famous and wealthy friends. Anaïs immediately began working for him, answering his correspondence, translating and editing his writing. She was caught up in the whirl of Manhattan night life, theatre parties, luxurious dining, and the status conferred upon her by her association with Rank. In the meantime, both Hugo and Henry were becoming increasingly suspicious.

1935: NEW YORK, PARIS
THE PUBLISHING GROUP, FAREWELL TO RANK

On January 2, 1935, when Hugo arrived in New York, he and Anaïs moved to his family home in Forest Hills, and Anaïs continued to commute to Manhattan to work for Rank. Their affair was over (he disliked her deceptions, she his vulnerabilities), but their working relationship continued. In fact, when Rank was away from New York, from January to the middle of spring, Anaïs filled in for him, analyzing his patients.

Her final severance with him occurred during the annual psychoanalytic meeting in Long Island in June of 1935. Anaïs was disappointed by the dryness of the academic presentations and felt that the profession led to a fragmentation of living rather than a fulfillment. She had learned a great deal from Rank, including the recognition that her life was a process, that she need not feel guilty for her desire to create, and that her creative work was her writing.

On June 15, 1935, suffering from another bout of depression, Anaïs sailed for France with Hugo and spent the following six months frustrated and unhappy. She and Hugo closed up Louveciennes, which was unheated, to move to Paris for the winter. They rented an apartment in a very bourgeois and chic neighborhood, where Anaïs's sense of estrangement deepened even more. Early that winter, still struggling with her sense of place, she initiated a project with Henry, and two mutual friends, Fred Perlès, and Michael Frankel — a publishing group that would finance and find publishers for each other's work. When the men came up with a list of titles to be published, however, none of her work was included. She then insisted on her own writing, and prevailed. After many discussions, the group agreed first to promote Henry's *Black Spring*, followed by Anaïs's *House of Incest*.

1936: PARIS
THE APPROACHING WAR, GONZALO,
A HOUSEBOAT ON THE SEINE

In 1936, *House of Incest* was released in two hundred forty-nine signed and numbered copies, and its appreciative reception lifted Anaïs's spirits. She welcomed a particularly enthusiastic response from Stuart Gilbert, an English critic, and friend and translator of James Joyce. To celebrate her success, and to debut a new apartment she and Hugo moved into, they threw a huge housewarming party in early July of 1936. Among the guests was a Peruvian couple, Helba Huara and Gonzalo Moré. Anaïs had heard about them from several friends as an extraordinary pair: the woman, a former dancer, the man, a musician and Marxist. From the moment she laid eyes on him, Gonzalo became the new romance in Anaïs's life.

Gonzalo was tall, handsome, and completely indifferent to the arts, unless they had direct political application. Though it was not obvious to Anaïs at first, he also was an alcoholic and virtually unable to act on his political convictions. Helba had been a successful dancer, but began going deaf, then succumbed to a variety of other real and imagined illnesses, controlling Gonzalo with her dependence. Because neither of them worked, they lived in poverty in a tiny basement apartment often shared with their revolutionary friends. Anaïs's relationship to Gonzalo and Helba resembled the earlier triangle among Anaïs, Henry, and June, with Anaïs first feeling sympathetic toward the wife and then competing with her for the attention of her husband.

To pursue an affair with Gonzalo, Anaïs rented a houseboat along the quai des Tuilleries. Hugo had no trouble believing she needed the solitude of her own place to write, and agreed to take on the added expense. During the summer of 1936, Anaïs juggled relationships with Hugo, Henry, and Gonzalo, writing, and promoting her work. Through the year, Henry's notoriety continued to grow, as did the number of his admirers, including the young writer Lawrence Durrell, with whom he and Anaïs began a lively correspondence. Though Anaïs criticized him for needing to live at the center of his worshipers, his success also inspired her own work. She began copying parts of the diary for the literary agent, Denise Clairouin, with the hope of future publication.

1937: PARIS
THE THREE MUSKETEERS OF LA COUPOLE

Just before Anaïs's thirty-fourth birthday, feeling productive and well-loved, she described her life as a dance. Hugo had accepted a position with the bank that required him to live in London during the week, giving Anaïs all the freedom she wanted to be with Henry or Gonzalo. When the publishing house of Faber and Faber reported to Denise Clairouin that they could not shape Anaïs's diary into an appropriate form for a book, Anaïs redoubled her efforts to transform diary entries into novels and short stories.

In July of 1937, Anaïs's rented houseboat was sold, forcing her into a more precarious position in dealing with her lovers. Another event also occurred that summer that was to be very important to her artistic development. Spotting an ad for a printing press for sale, she decided to buy it and install it in a small studio, presumably for Gonzalo to print his political tracts. It soon became obvious, however, that Gonzalo's idea of work was to sit in cafés all day, drinking and talking with friends. Almost by default, Anaïs taught herself to use the press, and surprised herself by how much she enjoyed the physical labor of laying out the type. Having the press gave her confidence, independence, and security. If publishers would not accept her work, she would publish it herself.

Late that summer, Lawrence and Nancy Durrell arrived in Paris to meet Henry and Anaïs for the first time. Curiously, Durrell was one of the only important men in Anaïs's life to whom she was not sexually attracted, or with whom sex was not a primary part of their relationship. It was almost as if she and Henry experienced Durrell as the child they had never had — their literary child. The three writers, who referred to themselves as "The Three Musketeers of La Coupole,"[38] sparked in each other an energetic chemistry that influenced each in a positive and productive way:

> Arguing with Henry and Larry helps her to reconcile in part her own struggle with the differences between male and female, between creating and nurturing. What emerges in her position is a call for "wholeness" of the artist, by which she means a recognition of the artist's feminine, intuitive side.[39]

In October of 1937, Henry published his essay about Anaïs's diary, "Une Être Étoilique," in T.S. Eliot's journal, *Criterion*. Both Anaïs and Henry wrote glorious reviews of Durrell's *The*

Black Book. And in December, Anaïs's story "The Paper Womb," later published as "The Labyrinth," appeared in the journal *The Booster,* alongside Henry's "The Enormous Womb," and Dylan Thomas's "Prologue to An Adventure."

1938 - 1939: PARIS
THE WAR INTRUDES

The time between the wars was about to end. Bloody civil conflict had erupted in Spain and the political unrest spreading throughout Europe was palpable. Anaïs wrote that in a destructive world, she was committed to providing a place of refuge, wholeness, and creativity.

In the summer of 1938, she also became involved in Maruca's divorce from her father. Both parties beseeched her to mediate their adversarial negotiations:

Reading Anaïs's description of her father's predicament, the reader is struck with Joaquin Nin's blind selfishness: only worried about who will take care of him and whether he will get to keep the maid, he is puzzled about why Maruca has changed, why she is divorcing him.

The reader is also struck by the parallel situation between father and daughter: years of unfaithfulness, almost flaunting one's affairs to court discovery; a "collector's need" of charm, conquest, and power; seduction under the pretense of altruism. That Anaïs is aware of the painful parallel is evident in her description of his infidelities: His do not come from "a love need" or a "real hunger," nor from "a natural, a primitive, warm-blooded impulse" (as presumably hers do). When Maruca rails against the selfishness and hypocrisy, Anaïs suggests that 'perhaps he did this to protect you from pain' — the reason she would continue to give for deceiving Hugo.[40]

The year 1939 was Anaïs's last in Paris. Hugo still was mostly in London, so he and Anaïs moved to smaller, less expensive quarters at 12 rue Cassini, for when he was home. Anaïs and Henry were spending much of their time together editing his new manuscript, *Tropic of Capricorn*, and correcting the proofs of Anaïs's *Winter of Artifice*, which was composed of three long stories: "Djuna," about Henry and June; "Lilith," about her father; and "The Voice," about Rank.

As Spanish refugees arrived in Paris, Anaïs worked with Gonzalo to help them find places to live. She also cooked big pots of soup to feed them, though it was against French law to aid illegal immigrants. The fighting in Spain affected her in another way, too. She was anxious about her own grand-mother in Barcelona, about whom she could not get any news.

Anaïs's last encounter with her father occurred during his final concert appearance in Paris, before his planned return to Cuba. In the middle of the performance, he suddenly collapsed onto the keyboard, motionless. Horrified, Anaïs ran to the stage. Joaquin Nin had had a minor stroke. Anaïs's spontaneous anguish when confronted with what had appeared to be her father's death forced her to realize how important he still was to her. When he sailed for Cuba she wept, knowing she had not resolved the love and hate she felt for him.

Anaïs and Hugo spent Easter of 1939 in Nice, where Anaïs was recovering from cosmetic surgery to correct her overbite and give her a more appealing smile. In May, the Durrells said their farewells and left Paris to return to Corfu. Henry planned to leave Paris in early summer, first to visit the Durrells, then to continue on to New York. He begged Anaïs to marry him and go to Greece with him, but she demurred, hoping to be with him again in New York and insisting that she had made a mistake by marrying in the first place. Before leaving Paris, Henry wrote out a will and sent it to a lawyer friend in Baltimore, leaving everything to Anaïs:

I owe a lot to France... But I must add in the interest of truth that I owe nearly everything to one person: Anaïs Nin... Had I not met her I would never have accomplished the little that I did. I would have starved to death... It was A [sic] woman, Anaïs Nin, by whom I was rescued and pressured and encouraged and inspired.[41]

On September 1, 1939, Germany invaded Poland. At the time, Anaïs was in London with Hugo, who had been made managing director of the newly merged City Bank and Farmers Trust. Two days later, Great Britain and France entered the war. When Anaïs returned to Paris, the train she was on was filled with French soldiers. Images of death would not leave her, and she was again threatened by the longstanding specter of depression. She tried to inspire herself through Gonzalo's political fervor, but his inability to act only depressed her more. Feeling lost again and with a diminishing sense of place and purpose, she begged Hugo to ask for a transfer to New York. He did, and got it.

Thorvald had long since left Europe. Rosa and Joaquin had already returned to the States. In December of 1939, Anaïs and Hugo boarded a train for Portugal, where they caught a hydroplane to the Azores. In the dark of night, the hydroplane churned through rough seas, and finally took to the air, away from the carnage in Europe to its destination in Bermuda for refueling, and then to the United States.

It was December of 1939, the holiday season, when Anaïs and Hugo arrived in New York. Although most of the sixty volumes of Anaïs's handwritten diaries were in a bank vault in Paris, she arrived with her current volume and three publications to her name: *D.H. Lawrence, An Unprofessional Study*; *House of Incest* (a prose poem); and *Winter of Artifice* (a collection of fiction).

After fifteen years in Paris, she is still seeking public approval, an American audience, and acclaim as a writer. She will make America her last home, first in New York City and then Los Angeles, but it will take nearly three years for any publisher to pay attention, and fame will come only with the Aquarian generation some twenty-five years later.[42]

Almost immediately upon arrival in Manhattan, Anaïs contacted Frances Steloff of the Gotham Book Mart, to whom she and Henry had been writing and sending requests to carry their work. The Gotham Book Mart was to New York what Shakespeare and Company was to the Left Bank in Paris

— a gathering place for contemporary writers and a venue for their work. Steloff prided herself in providing a home for such controversial publications as Joyce's *Finnegan's Wake*. She became a great supporter of Anaïs and Henry, a trusted personal friend, and introduced Anaïs to a pantheon of New York publishers, writers, and artists.

1940 - 1941: NEW YORK
FROTICA, GREENWICH VILLAGE DAYS

For much of February and March of 1940, Hugo was obliged to return to London on business. He was unaware that Henry had returned to New York to be with Anaïs, and assumed he was still in Greece. In early March, Gonzalo and Helba managed to get their papers in order and they, too, arrived in New York, seeking Anaïs's care. Anxious about her financial commitments to those who depended on her — her "children"[43] — as she called them, and wanting to make money of her own, Anaïs discovered a way to produce some much-needed income. She began writing erotica for a collector in Oklahoma. The man who provided the connection also gave her advice that proved invaluable. Long before the days of photocopying, he suggested she write with a carbon so she would have a copy of her work for editing or reproducing. *Delta of Venus* and *Little Birds*, Anaïs's best-selling erotica, were published from these carbons, and probably would not have existed without them.

In the fall of 1940, Anaïs and Hugo moved into an apartment near Greenwich Village. The literary history of the district and its small-town feeling helped Anaïs deal with the impersonal coldness she experienced in New York. So did sex. Anaïs wrote erotica each morning for the collector, and met privately with Gonzalo in the afternoons. As in Paris, she frequently felt overwhelmed by the demands of the people in her life: Gonzalo and Helba, Henry, and a growing circle of admiring young male writers. She did find the energy, however, to enjoy Harlem nightlife, and started an affair with the African American lover of one of her friends. Her venture into black culture also inspired her writing, and she fictionalized many of her encounters in her book *A Spy in the House of Love*.

Anaïs had begun to feel more at home in New York by the fall of 1941. She rejected pleas from Henry, then in California, to join him there. She became friendly with Greenwich Village neighbors including the sculptor, Noguchi; the composer, Edgar Varèse; and the engraver, Stanley William Hayter, who was renowned for using the techniques of William Blake. Hugo was so impressed with Hayter's work, he began studying engraving with him at the New School. The one remaining flaw was that she still was not being published.

1942: NEW YORK
THE GEMOR PRESS

In December of 1941, with a loan from Frances Steloff and another friend, Anaïs and Gonzalo bought a printing press, larger than the one she had bought in Paris, and found a loft at 44 MacDougal Street in which to house it. Tired of feeling like a literary outsider and angry that her work was not appreciated, she felt the press could be a solution to several problems at once. She could publish her own work, provide work and income for Gonzalo, publish Henry's work and provide him with more royalties than the other presses with whom he had published, illustrate the press's manuscripts with Hugo's engravings, and publish other writers at a fee that would bring regular income. Anaïs named the venture the Gemor Press — the first initial of Gonzalo's first name and his last name scrambled. She and Gonzalo worked long hours learning the intricacies of the huge manual press. On February 21, 1942, Anaïs's thirty-ninth birthday, she and Gonzalo set the first two pages of *Winter of Artifice* for what was to be a five-hundred-copy edition. It was illustrated with Hugo's copper engravings. They were attributed to Ian Hugo, Hugo's new nom d'artist.

In early May, the book was completed, and Steloff held a publication party at the Gotham Book Mart to celebrate. Anaïs and Hugo were both initially thrilled at the book's reception. But William Carlos Williams of *New Directions* then gave it a mixed review. Critiques in *The New York Herald Tribune Books* and in *The Nation* were somewhat negative, too. Anaïs found it difficult to tolerate the criticisms they included, experiencing them as personal attacks. Furthermore, sales of *Winter of Artifice* were slow, despite her hopes. The familiar cloud of depression again began to change the atmosphere of Anaïs's life.

1943 ‑ 1944: New York
New Analyst, New Hope

⁓ After struggling to complete two huge printing jobs early in 1943, exhaustion and depression overcame her. At the suggestion of a friend, Anaïs called the psychoanalyst Martha Jaeger for an appointment. In her first meeting with Jaeger, Anaïs wept with relief at having found a compassionate listener. With Jaeger, Anaïs felt she had a competent mother who could help her understand the split between her need to be loved and what she believed she must sacrifice to be loved — her need to create. Yet even Jaeger was, to some extent, seduced by Anaïs into breaking the boundaries of the analytic frame. As the analysis progressed, the two women became involved socially. Jaeger and her husband sometimes were invited to parties of Anaïs's and Hugo's. Jaeger also sought advice from Anaïs regarding dress, hair styles, and diet, as well as her husband's affairs.

On February 21, 1943, Anaïs turned forty. One of her birthday gifts was 100 dollars from Henry, who was still living in California and whose finances had begun improving. With the money, Anaïs purchased paper to begin printing a collection of short stories. *Under a Glass Bell*, illustrated by Ian Hugo, made its premier on March 6, 1944 at the Wakefield Gallery. At first, Anaïs was disappointed when reviews were few, and those that did appear were mixed. Then, when she received a complimentary review by Edmund Wilson of *The New Yorker*, she was overjoyed. Wilson had great praise for her work and quoted passages from several stories.

In the spring of 1944, she felt hopeful and confident. She

and Henry continued a friendship and literary relationship, but had ended their long affair. Anaïs's analysis with Jaeger provided her with support, understanding, and guidance in respecting and taking seriously the complexities of her own artistic needs and goals. Feeling renewed, she began work on another novel. She was just entering public view as a writer, and seeking praise and acceptance of her work. Her peripheral, outsider status became a natural link with the younger generation of writers who were also struggling to make their voices heard. Many were young, attractive men. Though she did not have affairs with all of them, she was their archetypal Donna Juana, faithful to none so she could remain faithful to all.

Hugo, meanwhile, retired from the bank that year to become a full-time artist himself. His illustrations for the Gemor Press's publications had garnered positive attention. He also had become interested in working in film. Anaïs, who was still involved with Gonzalo, as well as a number of young lovers, found renewed vitality in her marriage, now that Hugh Guiler, the banker, was metamorphosing into Ian Hugo, the artist.

1945: NEW YORK
FIRST COMMERCIAL CONTRACT

〰️ Henry was ensconced in Big Sur, living a life of writing in the grandeur of the California coast. He had married again and was coming into his own financially. He sent Anaïs $1,000, which helped defray the costs of moving the press to a new location and converting it to more manageable linotype.

In his letters, he always encouraged her writing, urging her to publish her diary unedited, the raw, pure experience. But Anaïs, fearful of hurting and angering those she loved, and unable to release control of the image she projected to others, chose another route. She began a continuous novel about women's conflicts, called *This Hunger*. Her work on this manuscript consisted of a collection of stories about various women who, each in her own way, portrayed one aspect of the universal character of all women. Anaïs worked with focus and energy on the project, while continuing to manage relationships with Hugo, Gonzalo, and her most serious new lover, a young writer named Lanny Baldwin, who had left his wife and young children to be with her:

> She does not see these [characters] as separate women. Nor does she see the various intimate affairs she is juggling as a splitting or "separation" of herself. Her multiple characters, like her affairs, are "symphonic," a vast "gathering together."[44]

When the United States dropped the two atomic bombs on Japan in August of 1945 to end World War II, Anaïs felt the need to counter the savagery of the destruction, and began printing *This Hunger*. At the same time, Baldwin decided to return to his family. Anaïs was furious at his rejection and accused him of being conventional, relinquishing an opportunity for growth to comply with bourgeois standards. In the meantime, she continued work on *This Hunger*, or, as she called it, "distilling the diary,"[45] and surrounded herself with beautiful young men who accompanied her in an entourage wherever she went.

Anaïs finished *This Hunger* at the end of September. Edmund Wilson, whose review of *Winter of Artifice* had sparked so much hope in her, returned to New York from covering the war as a journalist. She began a brief affair with him, the literary father figure whose approval she craved. His essentially positive review of *This Hunger*, which appeared in the *New Yorker*, also contained some criticism regarding her craftsmanship and undeveloped characters, however. Anaïs first became angry, referring to Wilson as a dictator, then despondent and depressed. She had also been hurt and angered by Isaac Rosenfeld's review of *This Hunger* in *The New Republic*, where he stated her characters were "personifications of neurotic anxiety" and her psychoanalytical style was "inadequate."[46] In her diary, she defended her writing as visionary, a style that transcended the surface and reached a deeper truth.

In the winter of 1945, Anaïs met another young man, a wealthy, well-educated and influential young man, unlike most of the adolescents who surrounded her. His name was Gore Vidal. At the time of their meeting, Anaïs had been recently contacted by several publishers who expressed interest in her next novel. Vidal, who had just been hired as Dutton's youngest editor, offered Anaïs an advance of $1,000 and her first commercial book contract. Anaïs's relationship with Vidal began with great mutual respect, then progressed, developed, and unraveled. Vidal's later vituperative caricatures of Anaïs in his novel The Two Sisters and other works, caused her great pain.

1946 - 1947: New York, Los Angeles
Rupert Pole

〜 As 1946 began, however, Vidal and Anaïs were still close. They spent increasing amounts of time together, talking, editing each others' work, attending parties, and participating as actors in the films of their friend Maya Deren. Anaïs was also busily engaged in finishing *Ladders to Fire* for her contract with Dutton. It was a novel composed of two sections, "This Hunger" and "Bread and the Wafer."

Hugo was in Mexico, working on a film of his own in the early months of 1946, Anaïs had completed her treatment with Dr. Jaeger and was trying to separate from Gonzalo, who had lost so much money on the Gemor Press that they were forced to cut their losses and close it. Dutton released *Ladders to Fire* in the late fall of 1946, to mixed reviews. Then Rupert Pole came into her life.

On February 18, 1947, just three days before Anaïs's forty-fourth birthday, she stepped into an elevator on her way to a party. With her in the elevator was a young man who on that very day had turned twenty-eight. Both Rupert Pole and Anaïs later described this initial meeting as love at first sight. Rupert, the son of Helen Taggart (who later married Lloyd Wright, Frank Lloyd Wright's son) and actor and director Reginald Pole, had been working as an actor in New York, but decided to return to California to attend the forestry program at the University of California Los Angeles (UCLA). From their initial meeting in the elevator, Rupert and Anaïs were inseparable. They spent every moment they could together before Rupert's departure for California. Rupert begged

Anaïs to accompany him. She agreed, telling Hugo she was accompanying a friend to Las Vegas to obtain a divorce. The trip was a liberation for Anaïs. She and Rupert motored through the rolling hills of Virginia, on to New Orleans, and then to New Mexico, where Anaïs was enchanted with the huge sky and landscapes of the Southwest. In California, she was welcomed by Rupert's mother and stepfather, and responded to them as if she had discovered a new family.

Also that year, she visited Henry and his new wife and baby in Big Sur. The visit was uncomfortable for everyone, except perhaps, the baby. From that time on, she and Henry saw little of each other, though they continued to correspond.

1948 - 1949: East Coast, West Coast
The Death of the Father

During the late 1940s, Anaïs began keeping a locked file called the "Lie Box."[47] Though it is not entirely clear what this file contained, it is likely that it was a decoy, like the green and red journals of the 1930s, designed to prevent Hugo from discovering her affairs.

In the spring of 1948, Anaïs rejoined Rupert in Colorado, where he was visiting his father who was there to direct a play. After the visit, Rupert went to a forestry camp and Anaïs flew to Texas for a promotional lecture and book signing. There, Hugo joined her and drove her to Los Angeles for a gallery opening that featured his engravings.

Anaïs's life became increasingly complicated as she became more and more devoted to Rupert. She felt comfortable and at home with his artistic and well-educated family, and was certainly more comfortable in the warmth of southern California than the noise and dirt of Manhattan. It was Rupert's encouragement that gave her the resilience to sign with another publisher when Dutton rejected her novel about Gonzalo, *The Four-Chambered Heart*. By this time, Anaïs had created a substantial body of work: *The Four-Chambered Heart*, *Ladders to Fire* — the weaving together of the lives of three women, and *Children of the Albatross*, the tale of a muse and the young artists who needed her inspiration and sustenance. The dominant themes of all these pieces were the struggle for integration through self-exploration. The book to come, *A Spy in the House of Love*, dealt with a woman's search for the one man who could reach her core and unify her many selves.

In October of 1949, Joaquin Nin y Castellanos died at his home in Cuba. Anaïs had not seen him since his stroke in Paris, and had long ago thought she had come to terms with his impact on her life, but his death rekindled old conflicts.

1950 - 1953: NEW YORK, LOS ANGELES
LONGING FOR RECOGNITION

The lack of an appreciative public added to her sense of loss. *The Four-Chambered Heart*, received more attention than those preceding it, but some reviews lambasted her melodramatic style. This year was filled not only with disappointment, however. One event gave Anaïs a greater sense of freedom. The joint passport she shared with Hugo had expired and she applied for one in her own name. Rupert, who thought she was divorced — a belief that she chose not to correct — hoped this symbolic break with Hugo would bring Anaïs and him closer to marriage. What Rupert did not know was that the strain of two permanent and secretive relationships was becoming more and more difficult for Anaïs. Hugo's new interest in film making awarded him substantial praise, which also meant that he was traveling more. Occasionally, Anaïs, Hugo, and Rupert were in the same city simultaneously, and the juggling act Anaïs performed to keep the two men from meeting became precarious to maintain. Anaïs managed this sleight of hand primarily by keeping a post office box or a mail drop at the home of trusted friends and swearing confidantes to secrecy.

In February of 1951, Anaïs turned forty-eight. Her books were not selling well, she was no longer the young temptress of her Parisian days, and every six to eight weeks, she left one partner and crossed the continent, either by plane or car, to live a separate life with the other man who believed he was her only significant other. To help her sort out her anxieties, when she was in New York she began analysis with Dr. Inge Bogner, with whom she also found immediate rapport. Though Bogner was helpful to Anaïs, like her other analysts, she too, seemed to have flexible boundaries in her relationships with patients, and often invited Anaïs and Hugo to have dinner with her and her husband. While still working with Anaïs, Bogner also accepted Hugo as a patient and continued treatment with him for over forty years.

For Anaïs, the years from 1951 to 1953 were filled with efforts to publish, to be recognized, and to live life on "a trapeze"[48] as she called it. Then, shortly before her fiftieth birthday, on a plane en route from Los Angeles to New York, she experienced an excruciating pain in her right side and hip.

Early in the morning on January 29, 1953, surgeons at New York University Hospital removed an orange-sized tumor from her right ovary. Still recovering, she celebrated her fiftieth birthday with Rupert in California.

Her father had died, her mother was frail, and she felt it was time to reflect on her own life and growth. In a letter to Henry, she wrote that she had come to terms with the split between the all-giving mother and the all-consuming father, and she had decided that her major work was her diary. She was prepared to allow it to be published.

1954 - 1958: NEW YORK, LOS ANGELES
THE DEATH OF THE MOTHER,
TWO HUSBANDS, MANY SELVES

She worried about the moral implications of revealing the secrets of her life, concerned that her family would be hurt and she might alienate them forever. Meanwhile, the publishing community bestowed further rejection. None of the invited critics came to her book party for *A Spy in the House of Love*. The first reviews were lukewarm at best and some were hostile.

That August, shortly after Anaïs visited with her at her home in Oakland, California, Rosa Culmell Nin died of a heart attack. Feeling remorse and guilt for never really reconciling with her, Anaïs began work on *Solar Barque*, which was first published in 1955, and again in 1959 as part of *Seduction of the Minotaur*. It was a story about a woman whose mother died, leaving her a sewing machine and a golden thimble (which Rosa had left Anaïs). In the story, the daughter passed into the mother's being for a year, taking on her characteristics and feelings.

Though Anaïs lectured and gave readings during 1954 and early 1955, the burden of her peripheral literary stature continued to depress her. Her analyst, Bogner, urged Anaïs to become more truly independent of Hugo, both emotionally and financially. Anaïs was not ready. She continued her arc across the States from one man to another.

Returning with her from a vacation in Mexico in the spring of 1955, Rupert brought up a subject that had been a continual source of tension between him and Anaïs: marriage. Because he was under the impression Anaïs was divorced, he rejected one by one all her reasons and excuses not to marry him. As the couple was driving through Quartzite, Arizona, Anaïs finally relented, never imagining that Rupert would immediately locate the justice of the peace, prepare the paperwork, and triumphantly announce that their wedding was to take place the next day. It did, as Anaïs confided to her diary:

> I exhausted all the defenses I could invent: That I was neurotic, that I did not want marriage, that I wanted to stay as we were, that I wanted to protect him from a feeling of responsibility, etc. To no avail. I know the persistence of his obsessions. I also feel tired of resisting, feared the effect of my frustrating him, felt also an ironic mockery of the laws, a feeling that if this had to be a source of irritation and insecurity, oh well, to hell with laws, I would gamble once more, one more gamble ... and gamble on the consequences.[49]

Now she was not only a married woman leading a double life with another man, but a bigamist. The marriage caused her increasing guilt, while mourning for her mother still occupied her waking and dreaming hours. She also was plagued by nightmares about being discovered and exposed by Rupert, Hugo, and her mother. In California, she took sedatives, and in New York she took "vitamin" injections (of steroids and amphetamines) from the later infamous Dr. Max Jacobson, better known as "Dr. Feelgood,"[50] who also treated Truman Capote, and Jacqueline Bouvier Kennedy and President John F. Kennedy.

In 1956, Anaïs found the energy to work both on her fiction and diaries, but was disheartened by the public acclaim of such work as Françoise Sagan's *Bonjour Tristesse*, which she found shallow. One piece of literature that gave her hope for her own work was Marguerite Young's *Miss MacIntosh, My Darling*. She was impressed by Young's integration of the inner and outer life, the necessary combination of conscious and unconscious realities.

In the fall, a new infusion of young writers entered Anaïs's life when she attended a reading in Hollywood of two young Beat poets, Allen Ginsberg and Gregory Corso. Always inspired by young talent, Anaïs responded to the vitality of these two young men and was reminded of her early days in Paris. Before the turning of the year, Anaïs received some encouraging news. The Avon edition of *A Spy in the House of Love* had healthy advance sales, raising her hopes of again breaking through the barrier of public acceptance of her work.

Back in New York in 1957, Anaïs infused her analysis with Dr. Bogner with new energy. One of the primary topics was

Anaïs's inability to integrate her life and live faithfully with one man. Bogner helped her reach a deeper understanding of her father's early abuse and how it had colored every relationship with the need to seduce and control lest she be abandoned again. Bogner helped Anaïs investigate how, in order to make meaning of her early abuse and abandonment, she had turned to writing to organize and transform the emotional chaos. Her connection to Bogner and their explorations helped Anaïs to embark on a new project: reprinting her books, insisting that they not be consigned to oblivion. That year she reprinted the continuous novel as a collection entitled *Cities of the Interior*, which included *Ladders to Fire*, *Children of the Albatross*, *The Four-Chambered Heart*, *A Spy in the House of Love*, and *Solar Barque* and found a new distributor for her books with Avon.

In the summer of 1958, Anaïs took a break from her work and accompanied Hugo on a tour of Europe to show his films and exhibit his engravings. In France, she met the writer Jean Fanchette, who helped her find a French publisher. She also had an emotional reunion with Lawrence Durrell. After Hugo returned to New York, Anaïs stayed on in Paris, where Rupert joined her for a five week automobile tour of France, Italy, and Spain.

Returning to California, Anaïs had two unwelcome discoveries. She was not included in a number of anthologies that had seemed promising and the Kinsey Institute announced it had purchased the erotica she wrote for the collector in the 1940s, which was rumored to have been excerpted from her diaries.

1959 - 1964: New York, Los Angeles
New Friendships, Building a Home

⌒ In March of 1959, in New York, Anaïs suffered a near-fatal bout of double pneumonia for which she was hospitalized for ten days. Though she had made a full recovery, she found herself feeling anxious and fatigued. Still, her creative energies were fully engaged in her role as the New York editor of Jean Fanchette's new journal, *Two Cities: La Révue Bilingue de Paris*. Her contributions to it were her first pieces of original work to be published in ten years, and she was once again optimistic that her literary identity was quickening.

During 1959, Anaïs became somewhat disenchanted with Rupert. Her life with him was filled with the everyday realities of domesticity, rather than the bohemian glamor of the creative milieu. Furthermore, he had changed professions. Having become dissatisfied with forestry, he obtained a teaching certificate, and was now a high school science teacher, a job that seemed mundane to Anaïs. Even though he had recently purchased a piece of land above the Silver Lake Reservoir and was building a house with plans drawn up by his half-brother, Eric Wright, Frank Lloyd Wright's grand-son, she began to feel that Hugo had more depth and artistry. To gain perspective and take a break from Rupert, Anaïs spent the summer of 1959 traveling through Europe with Hugo.

By winter of 1960, Anaïs was back in her new Los Angeles home with Rupert, her feelings for him rekindled. The house was small, but its many windows, simple, almost Japanese lines, and use of open space gave it a feeling of fluidity and comfort. Outside, the gardens provided privacy and hid the swimming pool from observation. The pool itself was a wonderful creation, unlike the turquoise rectangles that dotted southern California. Rupert had designed a pool for Anaïs that was shaped like a natural forest pond. It had a dark green bottom, making it even more like a natural body of water.

Though Anaïs was enamored of her new environment and Rupert's unwavering love, 1960 became a year of increased travel for her. Needing to augment his income, Hugo had begun working as an independent investor, which required a great deal of travel but also provided him and Anaïs with the opportunity to present his films and etchings and her writing to a larger audience in the states and in Europe.

After years of feeling adrift in the world of publishing, in 1961, Anaïs found a secure home for her writing in the person of Alan Swallow and the Swallow Press. Anaïs had first met Swallow in Denver in 1947 when she and Rupert drove across the country. For the past half-dozen years, Swallow had run a press dedicated to avant-garde work. When Anaïs contacted him regarding publishing her writing, he was immediately enthusiastic. Serious and creative, he read everything Anaïs sent him, and proceeded to organize her writing according to theme and development.

That same year, Henry Miller became a wealthy and controversial figure with the American publication of *Tropic of Cancer*. Now living in Pacific Palisades with his fourth wife, he was embroiled in obscenity suits over the book that eventually went to the Supreme Court, and that he won in 1964.

In 1962, Anaïs went to visit him again. The former lovers and old friends had not seen each other for fifteen years. One reason for the visit was that Anaïs was anxious to retrieve her letters to Henry, which had been bequeathed to the UCLA library with the rest of his papers and documents. Her wish to retrieve them was to protect the secrecy of their relationship, which was not accurately documented until after both their deaths. Henry agreed to exchange her letters to him, for his letters to her, which were published in 1965 as *Letters to Anaïs Nin*.

In the early to mid-1960s, as Anaïs spent more and more energy editing and distilling her past diaries for publication, her current volumes became less and less important:

> By the mid-1960s, as she learns to make the transition from herself to others, and as she learns to edit her earlier diaries (without revealing compromising facts about her sexual life), her "current" diary dies. She later admits that she has "retired" from her own diary and is writing a "journal of others."[51]

Anaïs's sixtieth birthday, February 21, 1963, brought further anxieties about public acceptance and her own physical aging. Though she could not force acceptance of her work, she could fight the signs of aging. In the spring of 1963, she had a face lift. She also sought new friends. They included Christopher Isherwood and Alan Watts, who shared a houseboat in Sausalito, California with collage artist and painter Jean Varda, to whom Henry had introduced Anaïs years before. The decade of the 60s was also filled with experimental drug use, particularly psychedelics, which Anaïs had tried once in 1955 under the care of Oscar Janiger, who was involved in experimenting with mind expanding drugs and psychoanalysis. Though Anaïs had compassion for those who used drugs to search their souls, she felt that psychoanalysis and art were far more reliable and profound methods of reaching enlightenment.

Whatever her conflicts about Rupert had been, by 1964 she was spending more of her time with him in California. Though she still maintained two homes and two marriages, she seemed to have settled more contentedly into her relationship with him. Her publishing plans were in full bloom as 1964 began. She had been working diligently on a collection of short stories, *Collages*, and was also planning, with her New York agent and editor, Gunther Stuhlmann, for the publication of her correspondence with Henry and the edited volume of her diary that dealt with her years in Paris from 1931 to 1934. By autumn, Anaïs had transformed her passionate, adulterous, and creative days in Paris with Henry to a streamlined and highly edited account that omitted the fact of her marriage and Hugo's financial support and suggested only the remote possibility that she and Henry were more than literary companions. Because the project was too large for Alan Swallow to manage alone, he arranged for Harcourt, Brace and World to publish it.

1965 - 1974: New York, Los Angeles
Recurring Illness, Continuing Deceptions

As the publication of the diary drew closer, Anaïs became more and more worried and again began experiencing nightmares and episodes of guilt:

The crisis of public scrutiny threatens the "protective cave" of her journal in which she has hidden (while giving the impression of revealing confession). This 1965 period, until the spring of 1966, is marked by great ambivalence. Though she claims that after years of analysis, she has put to rest her anxiety and is now relaxed, she continues to fly between the two coasts, with all the excuses, lies, and tensions this entails.[52]

In late October, while working in New York, Anaïs suddenly fell ill. She was hospitalized and had surgery on November 4th, 1965, awakening to learn that she had had a hysterectomy.

She returned to Los Angeles as soon as she recovered from the surgery, but the next spring she again became ill and had a second operation. She was not informed of the truth. She had cancer.[53] The galleys of the diary were brought to her in the hospital to edit so she would not miss her publication date of April 20th. *The Diary of Anaïs Nin (1931-1934)* was released in April of 1966. The response to it made up for a lifetime of rejection. During the first year after publication, the diary received more than thirty-six major reviews, none of which attacked and criticized her in the devastating manner with which her fiction had been reviewed. Though there was some critical commentary, it could not stand up to the overwhelming number of personal letters and support Anaïs received. Admirers wrote to her of the many ways in which she had changed their lives by her courage and independence. Before the first volume was released, Anaïs began preparing the second, covering 1934-1939, which appeared in 1967. The years 1969, 1971, 1974, and 1976 each ushered into the publishing world another volume of Anaïs's extensively edited diaries.

With her publishing success came a substantial change in her financial circumstances. She was now earning an income, both from advances for future publications and from royalties. Her popularity as a lecturer provided her with the opportunity to engage in her passion for travel. In 1967, she and Rupert visited Tahiti, Mexico, Morocco, and Japan.

One problem that Anaïs's increase in income caused, however, was that she had two husbands, both of whom assumed that they were to be claimed as dependents on her income tax returns. In the past decade, Hugo's finances had become shakier than ever. Though he possessed a sound business instinct, he had made some risky private investments to devote himself fully to the costly art of film making. Unfortunately, none of the schemes materialized. Anaïs believed her only hope of recovering her financial stability was to confess the truth to Rupert. She convinced him that Hugo would never have been able to survive a divorce, and that she was devoted to Rupert, and had married him purely out of love. She explained that because she had, in fact, been married to Hugo at the time of her marriage to Rupert, it had never been legal. To keep from being investigated by the Internal Revenue Service, she begged him to accept a legal annulment. She also explained that her sexual relationship with Hugo had ended when she met Rupert, that she and Hugo had separate bedrooms in New York, and that it would be criminal to abandon him now, when his health was failing and he needed her. Rupert agreed, and even felt that Anaïs's desire to aid her ailing husband was proof of her altruism. So, on June 16, 1966,

Anaïs's marriage to Rupert was officially annulled.

This was a time of success and gratification. The publication and positive reviews Anaïs was receiving opened a new circle of friends and associates. She also received many invitations to lecture, read, and sign books, which gave her the opportunity for further travel, including trips to Greece and Morocco, as well as an appearance in 1969 at the Frankfurt Book Fair, and a press tour to Paris. She also suffered a major loss. On Thanksgiving Day, 1966 Alan Swallow died. A grieving Anaïs flew to New York to bid farewell to the man who had championed her work.

Early in 1970, her own health worsened. Rupert convinced her to consult a doctor. She had been suffering from vaginal bleeding for more than a week. Tests revealed that she had inoperable cancer. This time the doctors told her their diagnosis. Not satisfied with the verdict, she flew to New York to consult with her regular doctor, who assured her the tumor had not metastasized and that radiation treatments would keep it in check. For three weeks, she dutifully appeared at the hospital where her pelvic area was bombarded with a high dose of radiation. When the treatments were over, she immediately returned to California and Rupert to recuperate. Before the year was over, she went to London for the publication of the third volume of the diary (1939-1944), then to Paris to publicize the French translation of the second volume (1934-1939). The flurry of lectures, readings, writing, and editing that Anaïs accomplished from ages sixty-seven to seventy-four was informed by her knowledge that time was against her. Of the honors she was awarded during these years, perhaps the most important was the French Prix Sévigné for the first two volumes of the diaries. She also was granted honorary doctorates from Philadelphia College of Art in 1973 and Dartmouth College in 1974.

In spring of 1973, she and Rupert, together now, at least half the time for almost twenty-five years, vacationed in Mexico. Since her radiation treatments, she had had trouble with her digestion and had recently again begun to experience light vaginal bleeding. Still, in 1974, she and Hugo traveled to Paris, he to promote his films and she to promote her books. Upon returning to the States, she remained for a short time with him in New York, then returned to Los Angeles.

1975 - 1977: LOS ANGELES
GROWING APPRECIATION, FAILING HEALTH

In mid-December of 1974, Anaïs again became seriously ill. The bleeding had increased and she was in terrible pain. Rupert rushed her to Cedars-Sinai Medical Center, where she remained from Christmas 1974 to March 7, 1975. In January, she underwent surgery that prolonged her life, but left her feeling psychologically and physically mutilated. The procedure necessitated a colostomy.

Knowing that time was limited, Anaïs had all two hundred fifty volumes of her diaries, which had been in storage in New York, shipped to Los Angeles where she hoped to find a permanent home for them. UCLA arranged to purchase them, but for tax reasons could not do so until after her death. By the end of 1975, Anaïs was again back in the hospital, as she would be on and off for the remainder of her life. When she could, she worked on editing her childhood diary, which was published in 1978 as *Linotte*, continued to meet with several of her writing students, and visited with friends. One of the final tributes she received was being chosen as one of the *Los Angeles Times's* 1976 Women of the Year. She was too ill to attend the ceremony and receive the award herself, so her friend Christopher Isherwood accepted it on her behalf.

During the last months of her life, she wrote a letter to Hugo asking him to absolve her. Hugo responded, granting her request, though he claimed not to understand fully what she meant. She also asked Rupert to help her place a call to Hugo, who was at home in New York. After a marriage of almost fifty-four years, she wanted to say goodbye.

In the final weeks of her life, the morphine that was necessary to dull her pain also made her less aware and alert. Rupert remained devoted to her every need. He agreed with her wish to die at home. He rarely left her side. When her pain grew unbearable in spite of the morphine, however, he became worried and took her back to the hospital. On January 14 at 11:55 p.m., Anaïs Nin died.

The following morning, Rupert called her brother Joaquin to tell him the news. Joaquin notified Hugo. According to Anaïs's wishes, she was cremated:

I [Rupert] took her ashes aloft in a small plane over Santa Monica Bay. I had studied the navigation charts carefully. All the markings were described by ordinary fish names except one. Mermaid Cove. I told the pilot to fly there, and I let go of the blanket containing her ashes just as a ray of sunlight broke through the overcast sky.[54]

EPILOGUE

For many years after her death, Anaïs's popularity grew. She was becoming an icon for a generation of young women who were seeking guidance and inspiration during a time of shifting cultural mores and roles.

Then the unedited volumes of her diaries were published. The first, in 1986, was *A Literate Passion / Letters of Anaïs Nin and Henry Miller 1932-1953*. Many of her readers felt betrayed. Anaïs, model of strength and courage, who presented herself as having lived an independent life dedicated to writing and encouraged her young followers to do likewise, had, in fact, been emotionally and financially dependent. Subsequent releases of the unedited diaries revealed further discrepancies. Literary and personal criticism increased.

In the confusion there remained many questions. What had caused her to keep secrets, create lies, invent herself over and over again with relentless dedication?

The following analysis discusses the causes and consequences of Anaïs's secrets and revelations.

NOTES: PART 11—A BRIEF BIOGRAPHY

1. Nin, A., (1966), p. vii.
2. This biography is based on the well-researched and thoughtful biographies by Noel Riley Fitch, (*Anaïs, The Erotic Life of Anaïs Nin*, 1993), and Dierdre Bair, (*Anaïs Nin, A Biography*, 1995) and my personal communications with Anaïs and Rupert Pole.
3. Bair, D., 1995, p. 15.
4. Anaïs Nin, personal communication, March, 1969.
5. Nin, A., 1978, p.3.
6. Ibid., p. 410.
7. Ibid., p. 105.
8. Ibid., p. 58.
9. Ibid., p. 144.
10. Ibid, p. 184.
11. Ibid, pp. 231-232.
12. Fitch, N.R., 1993, p. 40.
13. Bair, D., 1995, pp. 40-41.
14. Ibid., p. 47.
15. Nin, A., 1982, p. 232.
16. Bair, D. 1995, p. 533.
17. Fitch, N.R., 1993, p. 46.
18. Nin, A., 1982, p. 430.
19. Ibid., pp. 445-446.
20. Fitch, N.R., 1993, p. 53.
21. Ibid., p. 64.
22. Nin, A. 1983, p. 208.
23. Fitch, N.R., 1993, p.75.
24. Bair, D., 1995, p. 83.
25. Fitch, N.R., 1993, p. 76.

26. Bair, D., 1995, p. 100.
27. Nin, A., 1959, p. 27.
28. Fitch, N.R., 1993, p. 98.
29. Bair, D., 1995, p. 117.
30. Stuhlmann, G., (Ed.), 1987, p. 16.
31. Bair, D., 1995, pp. 131-132.
32. Ibid., p. 133.
33. Fitch, N.R., 1993, p. 133.
34. Ibid., p. 150.
35. Ibid., p. 168.
36. Nin, A., 1992, pp. 373-375.
37. Nin, A., 1945, p. 119.
38. Fitch, N.R., 1993, p. 211.
39. Ibid., p. 209.
40. Ibid., pp. 214-215.
41. Ibid., pp. 219-220.
42. Ibid., p. 224.
43. Nin, A., 1969, p. 100.
44. Fitch, N.R., 1993, p. 266.
45. Ibid., p. 270.
46. Ibid., p. 275.
47. Bair, D., 1995, p. 360.
48. Ibid., p. 340.
49. Ibid., p. 373.
50. Fitch, N.R., 1993, p. 333.
51. Ibid., p.360.
52. Ibid., p. 371.
53. Bair, D., 1995, p. 616, note #2. Anaïs's medical records were sealed after her death. Her precise diagnosis is not known.
54. Fitch, N.R., 1993, p. 410.

Part III

⌒

Understanding Anaïs

If the artist (in whatever medium) is searching for the self, then it can be said that in all probability there is already some failure for that artist in the field of general creative living. The finished creation never heals the underlying lack of sense of self.

— D.W. Winnicott[1]

⌒ This quotation refers to the result of early trauma on a developing child, and how such a child then becomes an adult deprived of a sense of authenticity, and is handicapped in the free expression of innate creativity. It could have been written with Anaïs in mind.

Because Anaïs kept journals from early adolescence to the end of her life, in her very first journal, *Linotte*, we have a unique window into her childhood psychology and how the unresolved issues of her youth influenced her later development as a woman and a writer. *Linotte* was friend, confidante, mirror, memory. It was originally composed of seven hand written volumes, and was published in 1978, a year after her death.

Who Anaïs was in *Linotte* was who she became. The contents of this early journal and Anaïs's relationship to it exemplify the psychological principles that played out in various ways for the duration of her life. The primary among these were Anaïs's fundamental beliefs that she was unlovable to her father and burdensome to her mother. Her life was a constant battle to disprove these beliefs and to ward off the depression, anxiety, fear of rejection, and self doubt that were their legacy.

As is true for most traumatized children, Anaïs adapted to and accepted her situation as best she could. Like a tree that has survived a blight and grown around an infestation in its roots, so did Anaïs survive, with the scars of her childhood invisible but powerfully affecting her later development. Her simultaneous sexual liaisons, deceptions, multiple personae and need to control others' good opinions of her were the observable manifestations of her childhood that garnered her both reverence and derision. But what is of far greater importance than the litany of her exploits are the motivations for them.

Overall, Anaïs's childhood left her with tremendous doubts about her intrinsic value and lovability. These issues translate more specifically into difficulties she had throughout her life in managing intermittent depression and anxiety, establishing an authentic sense of self, relinquishing control, distinguishing between internal and external reality, and being able to use her resources in the service of uninhibited creativity.

Linotte begins the record of Anaïs's efforts to come to terms with her past, her present, her future, and most importantly, with the disparity between who she was and who she wanted to be:

December 31, 1919

It is 11. Maman is in bed; so are Thorvald and Joaquinito. I am writing — the two of us [Anaïs and her diary] are waiting for the New Year!

How many things there are that no one can write, no one understand! Tonight I am troubled by many different feelings, for as I realize a New Year is about to begin, I have been going over the old one ... Many people generally spend the few hours before midnight making resolutions and promises. I promise nothing; I have such a weak character that I can't promise to be better, but God knows how much I want to be, with what enthusiasm and will power. I want what is best in me to live. But I know that I have very few things to ask for just now, compared to the infinite number of things for which I should give thanks ...[2]

It is generally accepted that Anaïs began her diaries as a letter to her absent father, hoping to present such a compelling portrayal of her life and her need for him, that he would be seduced into returning to her and the family. Until she was seventeen years old she wrote her diary exclusively in French, the language her father preferred. When she was seventeen, she made the switch to English because she and her cousin, Eduardo, began sharing their journals in their only common written language. By that time, Anaïs had also relinquished hope of her father's return.

What began as an enticement to an errant father became the essential creation of a lifetime. The theme of seduction began with the first volume and was woven through them all, through Anaïs's life and work, often blurring the boundaries between who she was and what she created. Seduction is an important defensive strategy. It is designed to protect an individual from the overwhelming trauma of disconnection from, or loss of, a crucially important relationship. Anaïs's need to be loved was often expressed by her attempts to please others, to seduce them with her beauty, kindness, generosity, and intelligence in an effort to win them over and make herself feel lovable. Because it was so difficult for her to believe that she could be loved for herself, she attempted to please others by trying to become what she perceived they wanted her to be.

In 1966, when *The Diary of Anaïs Nin, 1931–1934* first appeared, it was known that it and subsequent volumes of her diary were edited. Not until more than twenty years later, with the publication of *Henry and June* (1986), *A Literate Passion* (1987), and *Incest* (1992), was the extent of the omissions made clear. Anaïs not only edited her diaries with publication in mind, she also omitted truths, bent reality, told "necessary lies," or "mensonges vitals"[3] and intentionally, or, perhaps, reflexively, fashioned an idealized self to present to her readers.

The obvious theme of seduction in Anaïs's life is evident in her history of multiple, simultaneous sexual relationships. The less obvious seduction has to do with her needs, conscious and unconscious, to combat her childhood abuse and rejection by creating a self, or seducing into being through an act of will, a creature of such perfection that she would be adored by all, rejected by none, and triumph forever over loss and abandonment. Though Anaïs sought to win the admiration and adoration of others, her main target was herself. Her motivation was to seduce, charm, win over, and transform the unlovable person she experienced herself to be in the only way she imagined possible — to love herself through others' love for her. Like Pygmalion's Galatea, the perfect woman would be born of artistic inspiration. Except that in Anaïs's case, art and artist would be one, with the diary serving as blueprint for the creation of the ideal woman.

As Webster's defines "seduction" it is "to persuade (one), as into disobedience or disloyalty."[4] This definition implies being lured away from an allegiance, in Anaïs's case, an allegiance to the self, and insists upon a dynamic in which the self is forced to relinquish its own needs and real experience in order to remain connected to an all important other person. In the following excerpt from *Linotte*, a month before Anaïs's twelfth birthday, she describes her depression in being separated from her father, her assumption that she must hide her feelings so as not to inflict them on others, and her beliefs about why her father has not returned to her:

January 1, 1915

New Year! We didn't celebrate because Aunt Edelmira is still not quite well. We just went out for a walk and played. Everyone here keeps shouting all the time, Happy New Year! I have not forgotten Papa's absence... Papa's name alone, makes me dream for hours on end. Only my heart can explain how I feel, my pen cannot do it.

Perhaps my feelings are absurd, I think so and I shall stop. All that makes me feel like crying and I contain myself only with great difficulty. I can't explain this state of mind. Luckily I manage to conceal it and no one sees or guesses. If I suffer, I mustn't make the others suffer too. Besides, what good would it do? Would their sorrow help console me for mine? No, so only my diary has the right to suffer like me, to think like me, since its destiny is to hold my heart's most secret thoughts. To return to what we were saying, why does the thought of Papa make me so sad? Perhaps I want so much to have him near me, I want so much to give him a long, tender hug as I see the other children do. I cry because I think, who is it who keeps Papa from being here with me? Is there someone dearer over there who holds him back? How many times I have asked myself that question. I think that might be it, for I am just a silly girl, full of fancies, of crazy ideas, so I can understand that Papa might love an intelligent girl more, someone with the right kind of ideas who may have taken my place. Although I try to think it out and make myself understand that, I cannot accept it, I cry and get into the state of sadness that I have already explained to my diary.[5]

It is no wonder that as a young girl, Anaïs desperately sought some means by which to make sense of the chaos and pain to which she was continually exposed. Her father was verbally and physically abusive to his wife, to Anaïs, and to her two younger brothers. The children suffered beatings, rageful outbursts, and cutting insults at their father's whim. His sadism was random and terrifying. Other than disciplining the children, he had little to do with them when he was home. He remained aloof and irritated by their requests for attention and affection. When Anaïs was two years old and seriously ill with typhoid fever — so ill, in fact, that her life was in danger — his only response to her suffering was to comment on how ugly she had become.

Experiencing trauma, such as abandonment, illness, molestation, or abuse early in development, particularly prior to fluent language acquisition, often results in later interpersonal and identity problems. Because these insults occur before they can be verbally expressed, we frequently see their results in later forms of maladaptive behaviors, such as promiscuity, substance abuse, eating disorders, gambling, and other activities that are compulsive in nature and marked by a lack of impulse control. Because a child's first interaction with the world is physical, bound by the five senses, early traumas are typically more difficult to resolve than those that occur after verbal fluency has been established. Prior to language acquisition, there is no cognitive memory, no way to structure and communicate experience. Prior to language acquisition, there is only physical experience whose meanings are physiologically encoded in the body.

This need for symbolic communication was portrayed in the film, "The Miracle Worker," a dramatization about Helen Keller's childhood. In the film, Annie Sullivan (played by Anne Bancroft) had been hired by the Kellers to be Helen's tutor when Helen was about seven years old. Helen, (played by Patty Duke) had been a bright child who had begun talking when she was six months old. A few months later, however, she became ill. Though she was not expected to live, she did recover, but the illness left her blind and deaf.

By the time Helen was seven years old, she behaved like a feral animal in captivity. She was unsocialized, isolated, and without ability to understand and communicate experience. Annie spent many long hours attempting to teach Helen the manual alphabet for the deaf and blind. In this form of communication, letters and symbols are "spelled" into the recipient's open palm as the person communicating makes meaningful shapes with his or her hand. In the dramatic climax of the movie, after many exhausting failures, Annie drags a screaming Helen to the water pump in the yard to refill a pitcher she had spilled in a fit of temper. Helen holds the pitcher under the spout in one hand, and operates the pump handle with the other. The water flows into the pitcher and splashes onto her hand and arm. There is a moment, a pause. Annie pulls Helen's hand from the pump and spells out "water," repeating it again and again. Suddenly, Helen makes the connection between the water running through her fingers and Annie's hand in her palm, repeating over and over a recognizable pattern that has meaning — that means "water." In that instant, order has vanquished chaos. The sensory has been mediated by the cognitive, banishing isolation, welcoming connection and relationship.

Though few of us have had to endure Helen Keller's obstacles in making meaning out of experience, all of us who use language have had to make the transition from sensory experience to sensory-cognitive experience. Because language has few concrete qualities apart from written or tactile symbols, or sound, rhythm, and physical vibration, it is one of the most abstract and adaptive means of communication. Because of the malleability of language, meaning is assigned to words through the use of culturally accepted grammar and vocabulary. The qualities of language that imbue it with meaning provide the user with power to organize and thereby transform experience through the use of symbols. I refer to this process as the "Rumpelstiltskin Phenomenon," inspired by the German fairy tale about a dwarf, a miller's daughter, and the transformational power of language.

The tale of Rumpelstiltskin recounts the story of a prince who has fallen in love with the beautiful daughter of a local miller. The prince asks for the girl's hand in marriage, but only upon the condition that she spin a room-full of straw into gold. Unable to accomplish the task, but wishing to marry the prince, the girl begins to weep. Suddenly, she is surprised by the appearance of a nameless dwarf who offers to help her in her plight. His offer is conditional, however. She must agree to give the little man her first-born child if he will spin the straw into gold for her. The girl agrees to the arrangement. The dwarf spins the straw into gold, and the miller's daughter marries the prince.

A year later, the princess gives birth to her first child. She grieves so bitterly when the dwarf comes to fetch it that he is filled with pity for her and he agrees to forgive her debt if within three days she can discover his name. On the first two days, the princess flails about in her attempt to name the dwarf and offers hundreds of incorrect guesses. Determined not to lose her baby, she decides to send her trusted servant to spy on the dwarf in his forest home, hoping she will discover a clue to his secret identity. The servant does not have long to wait. At the stroke of midnight, the little man, certain of victory, lights a bonfire and begins to sing and dance around it, chanting, "Dream in peace, my royal dame, / Rumpelstiltskin is my name. / Other names you call in vain, / Rumpelstiltskin is my name." [6]

The next day, the dwarf appears at the castle, fully prepared to take the baby home with him. The princess approaches him and calls him, "Rumpelstiltskin." Upon hearing his name, the dwarf is so shocked, so filled with rage at having been discovered, that he disappears in a puff of smoke.

Though this story has many interpretations, including inferences about greed, gender roles, innocence, honor, and trust, the one that stands out psychologically concerns the power of language itself. It is only when the princess calls Rumpelstiltskin by his real name that his power is extinguished. It is through the use of language that the princess is able to identify a formidable and unnamed threat, stripping it of its grip and freeing herself from its spell.

The "Rumpelstiltskin Phenomenon" is not limited to millers' daughters, and it is often present in clinical work, for example, when a patient who has been suffering from bouts of weeping, loss of appetite, low energy, excessive sleepiness, and irritability is greatly relieved to discover that these afflictions are called depression, and that the constellation of symptoms described by this name can be treated. Naming the symptoms identifies them with an objective, external reality and situates them outside the patient's internal, subjective experience where repeated attempts to control and resolve them have failed. The power of language resides in our ability to use it to organize internal reality and communicate it to others through

4

Before Anaïs had full language acquisition to comprehend, organize, and communicate experience, she was overcome by physical illness and her father's frequent absences. Later, she was emotionally, physically, and perhaps sexually abused by her father. Eventually, when she was ten years old, he abandoned her, her mother, and brothers. Rationalizing his abuse and abandonment, Anaïs protected her idealized image of him by attributing his selfish preoccupation to his higher artistic nature. It might have proven a more manageable task for her to have dealt with a father who was only abusive and rejecting. But Anaïs's father was also seductive, and regularly flattered her with inappropriate sexual attention. This same critical, violent man took great interest in photographing his young daughter in the nude, caressing and exploring her body with his camera. These moments of intense interest necessarily were confusing for a young child. Though there is no record of paternal molestation, physical and emotional abuse, as well as her father's inappropriate sexual attention is considered by today's standards to be an intrusion on the developing self and a violation of body integrity. Anaïs's need as an adult to sexualize so many of her relationships, most dramatically, her incestuous relationship with her father, is congruent with current thinking on early father–daughter incest. What is certain is that the insufficient parenting Anaïs received interfered with her early development and served as a painful and restrictive template for her later artistic efforts and intimate relationships.

Just as Anaïs rationalized her father's behavior in order to protect her image of him, she also attempted to maintain an idealized image of her mother. In her mother's case, however, her efforts were directed towards creating a mother who was stronger and more resilient than Rosa really was. In *Linotte*, Anaïs describes her mother as patient, generous, loving, and, as her traditional Cuban Catholic upbringing dictated, devoted to the needs of her husband and children:

August 3, 1914
[Under a photograph of Anaïs's mother that had been pasted into the diary]
    You are looking at a great singer, my Maman. She has met with great success everywhere and, like Papa, she wears many laurel wreaths to reward her efforts. Besides being a great singer, she is devoted to us, more than any other mother in the world. Maman has a heart of gold, the kindness of her glance says so. I love her so much and she loves us deeply too, I know. My dear Maman does everything to give us pleasure, all her sacrifices are for us, she works only to assure the future for all of us. When I was sick, she was at my bedside day and night. Anything she could do to please me, she did, with never a second to herself. My dear Maman showed such kindness that I could never repay her by myself, but God will help me. She kisses me goodnight with so much sweetness, and without a kiss from my angel I couldn't even close my eyes. No mother on earth does more than Maman. Love, love to Maman, my dearest beloved angel.[7]

Rosa Nin was not only the sole caretaker of her children, but the family's primary financial support. It was mostly on

Rosa's family's money that the Nins lived during the first ten years of their marriage. Promoting Joaquin's concert career required a great deal of wealth. Rosa herself was a talented musician, a singer who had begun a satisfying performing and teaching career of her own. When she and Joaquin married, they planned to perform together until he was established well enough to draw audiences as a soloist. Rosa claimed it was her wish to give up her career in favor of domestic responsibilities, but her subservience to her demanding and publicly renowned husband later became an issue of great conflict in the Nin household.

Rosa proved to be a resourceful and competent provider for herself and her three children when her husband abandoned them in 1914, but was less able, however, to provide emotional support for herself and her family, suffering two breakdowns between 1919 and 1921.

Already burdened with the task of making emotional sense of her father's absence, Anaïs was further stressed by being the eldest child and the only girl in the family. Daughters of divorce or whose fathers have abandoned them frequently become over-identified and enmeshed with their mothers. They also consciously or unconsciously blame themselves for their fathers' rejection and often experience overwhelming anxiety about real or imagined abandonment. Though they long for intimacy, they are terrified by genuine closeness for fear that they will once again be abandoned. These women are frequently compelled by the pseudo-intimacy of multiple relationships or promiscuity, and substitute these for the real love and connection they fear they will never find or be able to keep.

Never confident that she was loved, Anaïs displayed an almost ethereal, other-worldly persona that reflected her lack of self-esteem, which in turn made her fearful about growing up, becoming independent, and functioning autonomously. As an adult, Anaïs has been criticized for being self-concerned, indulgent, and narcissistically preoccupied. In actuality, the development of these traits was an attempt to cope with insecurity. Such criticisms are gratuitous unless they are evaluated in the context that first brought them into being: the psychological impact of having been abused as a child.

When a child has been abused, when emotional and physical integrity have been violated, self-absorption or self-reflection become survival reflexes. With the fluidity of a gyroscope, an abused child constantly re-evaluates him or herself and makes appropriate adjustments to stay on course, attuned with and connected to the adults on whom the child is dependent. By constant self-monitoring, the child experiences a pseudo sense of control. The child cannot control the parent or caretaker and make him or her loving, but the child can attempt to control the self and make the self lovable. In this way, the child exerts an illusory control in an effort to stay connected to the beloved and necessary parent and, at the same time, wards off the dangers of loss or punishment that this person poses. Anaïs was anxiously preoccupied with maintaining just this type of control her whole life. After her first meeting with Henry Miller in the winter of 1931 she writes:

After he left, I destroyed my enjoyment, thinking he would not be interested in me, that he had lived too much, too roughly, too completely, like a Dostoevskian character, the lower depths, and he would find me inexperienced. What does it matter what Henry thinks of me. He will know soon enough exactly what I am. He has a caricatural mind I will see myself in caricature. Why cannot I express the fundamental me? I play roles too. Why should I care? But I do care. I care about everything. Emotionalism and sensibility are my quicksands.[8]

Though written seventeen years after she began her diary, the self-doubt she expresses in this selection is similar to the worries she expressed in *Linotte* as a child. Here, she assumes that she will disappoint Miller, laments the need to play a role to entice him, and acknowledges the difficulty in being herself.

It is a paradox that abused children such as Anaïs become exquisitely attuned to the slightest emotional nuances of the important love object, while also developing a hypertrophied capacity for vigilant self-reflection and self-preoccupation. In the service of making the self acceptable to the parent, and maintaining the parent as good at all costs, the child's relational world becomes a narrow and dangerous precipice from which he or she must never avert attention, for one false step could be catastrophic. For Anaïs, relentless self-inspection, self-criticism, and confession were the adaptive means to this end. Her self-absorption was a parody of self-love, expressing instead a symptom of pernicious insecurity in the face of the constant threat of losing those she loved.

Any abused and neglected child is placed in the difficult position of having to resolve two competing realities. The first is that the child loves and is totally dependent upon his or her parents. The second is that these parents are unreliable, even dangerous. Experiencing the self as bad or flawed, rather than experiencing parental deficits, gives the child the impression that with enough effort to be good, pretty, smart, kind, and so forth, he or she will be able to change the bad self into a good self, and be able win parental love and approval. This provides the child with a way to deny the objective horror of his or her abuse, and survive the desperation of his or her own helplessness. If the child were truly to comprehend the abusive treatment, the reality would be overwhelming and could constitute a serious threat to the child's sanity. Because a child is objectively, concretely dependent on his or her parents, he or she is literally helpless, at their mercy. Abuse in the context of helpless dependence is one of the most terrifying emotional states a human being can experience.

Assuming the reality of his or her own deficits also allows the abused child to comply with parental beliefs, paradoxically providing a way to be good by fulfilling their expectations. For example, imagine a teenaged girl, beginning to experiment with sex who is accused by her parents of being promiscuous. She may defend herself against such accusations, but if she cannot win her parents' understanding and respect, she may begin to fulfill their accusations and engage in forbidden behaviors. By so doing, she is both rebelling against their attempts to control her behavior and complying with their insistence that she is behaving badly. She simultaneously maintains her own integrity and identifies with their vision of her.

Anaïs's diaries enabled her to make a similar compromise between her perceived self and her idealized, wished-for self. She remained loyal to her perception of her parents' experience of her by faithfully recording and complying with their overt and covert criticisms of her. By documenting these flaws, however, she also attempted to create herself anew, to transform the disappointing and unlovable little girl into an ultimately desirable and perfect work of art. This necessitated constant self-reflection and evaluation, and is symptomatic of an impaired sense of authentic self and low self-esteem.

If Anaïs appears to be self-obsessed, narcissistic, or indulgent, as some critics have claimed, it is because the development of her spontaneous and authentic self was damaged and inhibited by the nature of the early trauma she endured. As a very young child, Anaïs experienced many intrusions that interfered with the development of a reliable sense of a true and authentic self. Her life-threatening bout with typhoid fever when she was two years old threatened any assumption of safety and protection she might have known. She sensed she was vulnerable and this perception was further validated by her later appendicitis and her relationship with her father, whose long absences and violent outbursts were just as unpredictable and equally beyond her influence to control.

When such unpredictable violence is chronic or acutely severe, the development of an authentic self is inhibited. The emergence of a false self is fostered because the child is forced to relinquish his or her own experience in order to maintain connection to the primary caretaker. The child who is in extended physical or emotional pain comes to expect that the mother, or primary caretaker, can not, or will not, respond to his or her needs. The child learns to accept whatever care is provided and attempts to be whatever he or she perceives necessary in order to maintain connection with the all important nurturer, however flawed that person may be. The true self, with its needs and perceptions is hidden, since its existence is not acknowledged and its needs are unmet.

The creation of a false self is an adaptive response to the threat of losing an essential relationship. It functions in much the same way a rhinestone necklace in the display window of a jewelry store might. The fake necklace appears convincing to most people, and they do not suspect that the real necklace, with its valuable and many-faceted stones, is protected from damage or theft in the store's safe. Like the false self, the decoy necklace serves to draw people's interest. Just as rhinestones would chip and scratch when put to the test, however, so the false self tends to disintegrate in the crucible of real intimacy and its demands for spontaneity, resilience, and adaptability.

The greatest problem with a false self is that it feels false to the individual employing it. These individuals often feel a sense of futility and unreality about their lives, and have difficulty finding meaning and satisfaction in their work and relationships. The false self is like an emotional chameleon, changing with the perceived demands of the environment in an effort to circumvent attack and rejection. In this way, the false self is a seductive self. It is an unconscious construction designed to protect the true self from danger while maintaining important relationships. Like a mask or a costume it is a presentation of a character for a role that is perceived as necessary for the maintenance of an important relationship and the prevention of rejection.

Anaïs lived much of her life as just such a protective false self. Her journals were the scripts she wrote to keep track of her many selves, as well as being the only place she felt safe enough to reveal her true self. In June of 1933, she writes:

This diary proves a tremendous, all engulfing craving for truth since, to write it, I risk destroying the whole edifice of my illusions, all the gifts I made, all that I created and protected, everyone whom I saved from truth.

What does the world need, the illusion I gave in life, or the truth I give in writing? When I went about dreaming of satisfying people's dreams, satisfying their hunger for illusion, didn't I know that this was the most painful and the most insatiable hunger? What impels me to offer now, truth in place of illusion?[9]

This selection typifies Anaïs's conflict between the compliant false self she feels she needs to present to others and her true self, which she fears will cause harm and disappointment, threatening her relationships.

The paradox of the false self is that its acceptance cannot be reassuring and comforting. In fact, it tends to exacerbate anxieties about authenticity and genuine relatedness. A child such as Anaïs, did not have parents who could competently respond to her needs for attention and affection. When she came to her mother for comfort or help, she received anxious attention about which she felt guilty. From her father, she received overt rejection or abuse.

In contrast, she received praise when she solved problems

alone, behaved independently, and made decisions on her own. This put her in quite a dilemma because revealing her needs made her vulnerable to feeling guilty or being rejected. At the same time, performing independently garnered praise, but did not address her real needs and longings. In order to maintain a precarious, positive connection to her parents, Anaïs had to strive constantly to be what she was not. The threat of exposing her true, needful self to potential rejection was too great a risk. Her parents' acceptance of her false self became the equivalent of their rejection of her true self. She then had to redouble her efforts to maintain connection while vigilantly protecting her true self from discovery and the traumatic threat of loss this would pose.

This self-reinforcing cycle continued into adulthood for Anaïs. It is a situation not unlike that in Edmond Rostand's story of Cyrano de Bergerac. Once Christian (representing the false self) is accepted, he has a tremendous investment in continuing the charade, anxiety about being discovered, and dependence on Cyrano for the success of his relationship with Roxanne. Cyrano (representing the true self), on the other hand, feels certain of Roxanne's rejection if the truth were exposed, is dependent on Christian for contact with her, and disheartened by the fruitlessness of his courtship by proxy.

Linotte introduces Anaïs's early efforts to come to terms with this dilemma of desperately wanting to be loved, and feeling profoundly unlovable:

November 23, 1916
    Today I am sad and in a bad humor. I am mean, really very mean. When maman scolds me, I am sorry and

I cry inside, but an insufferable pride makes me wear such a nasty air of indifference that Maman calls me "a bad lot." And heaven knows I suffer. A long time later I ask Maman to forgive me, but a voice still whispers in my ear that I was right.

I know that I am disorderly, lying, hypocritical, nasty and every bad thing there is in the world. I know I am the worst creature there is. I know that I deserve every imaginable suffering. I know that nobody loves me. I know that everyone criticizes me and scolds me, and then I feel this indescribable shame come over me. When I think about it, I hate myself and pour out a flood of tears, and yet my cruel pride holds me back and Maman never knows the regrets that I hide from her out of pride.

I would like to die right there when I see that Maman is angry with me, Thorvald runs away from me, Joaquinito makes fun of me, Godmother scolds me, and all that because I am bad, so so bad! I struggle with myself and I know I can't control myself because Maman is right when she calls me "Your father's own daughter!" I remember Papa's strong, unshakable, even stern disposition. There is something that I can't combat, and it hurts me terribly, oh! Yes, it hurts me so much![10]

The themes of vulnerability, wanting to be loved and accepted, self-discovery, and becoming independent are particularly intense in adolescence. In *Linotte*, we see how the normal anxieties of adolescence resonated for

Anaïs with her particular conflicts about being lovable and authentic. If the core, true self is experienced as deeply flawed and an individual is convinced of his or her lack of worth, being seen or exposed would be a humiliating and shameful experience, like the terrible exposure dreams of walking naked in a crowd.

In order to negotiate smoothly the transition between childhood and young adulthood, an individual must first feel securely attached, loved, and safely dependent. Feeling that he or she is loved, a child or adolescent can then feel free to come and go on his or her own terms, knowing that a welcoming parent will be available. It is much more difficult to separate successfully from a rejecting parent because of the threat of complete dissolution of the relationship. It is too great a danger, too great a risk, when separation may mean total severance.

It is also difficult to separate from a parent whom the child perceives to be wounded, weak, or damaged in some way, either physically or emotionally. In this case, it is not fear of losing the relationship that is inhibiting, but guilt at leaving such a depressed, ill, or incompetent parent behind.

It is clear that the childhood abuse and familial chaos Anaïs experienced interfered with her ability to discover and launch an authentic self. This was complicated by the additional burden of having to cope with a rejecting father and a depressed, critical mother. The disruption of Anaïs's resolution of this important developmental task raises questions about the integration of her sense of identity. Not only was she trying to win her father's love and approval, she also needed to negate her sense of guilt towards her mother. She did not have the emotional freedom to know herself for fear of harming her already overwhelmed mother and giving up all hope of her father's approval and return. She was caught in a painful double bind, where remaining connected to crucial relationships meant painful compromise, even coercive sacrifice of the self.

The ability for compromise is a developmental marker that is observable in the context of an individual's social and interpersonal life. It is predicated upon the development of a reasonably accessible true self. The individual who develops a predominantly false self organization is being asked to react to demands that have no internal counterpart and are therefore experienced as impositions or intrusions. A child such as Anaïs, who, at the age of two, became seriously ill and had only rudimentary language acquisition, cannot understand her suffering and has no internal analog with which to make sense of her pain and fear. A child in this position does not know the difference between feeling bad and being bad, because he or she has not yet fully completed the developmental task of recognizing the self and others as connected but separate entities. Add to this experience the constant fights between Anaïs's mother and father, her mother's anxiety and depression, and her father's violence, and we have a child who comes to expect the world to intrude upon her experience of herself chronically and painfully — a child who has no alternative but to comply.

This scenario contrasts dramatically with the experience of a healthy child of healthy, happy parents. If such a child is fearful, a parent comforts. If the child requires an appreciative audience a parent responds. The response the child receives from the external world corresponds with internal experience and promotes meaning and congruence between internal and external reality. For example, a prideful first step is met with applause. With such experience consistently repeated, the child comes to know external reality as benign, responsive, and complementary to internal reality. The experience of external reality corresponding to an individual's internal psychological apparatus provides a structure that the individual uses to organize experience and make meaning. The successful organizing of experience promotes a critical difference between an individual who is able to make compromises and one who feels that he or she must comply. Compromise is predicated on choice, compliance on coercion.

As with any traumatized child, coercion was an important dynamic in Anaïs's childhood. She had to comply with parental demands, direct and indirect. Because her traumas were not understood and resolved when she was a child, coercion remained an issue for her as an adult. She frequently felt obliged to do whatever she perceived as necessary to maintain important relationships, often feeling the need to lie and deceive, exhausting herself in the process.

In healthy development, parents are sensitive enough not to make demands before a child has the resources with which to organize experience and make authentic responses. If development continues without serious impediment, this individual will be able to decide when he or she wants to compromise in order to obtain something deemed particularly valuable. This give-and-take is not experienced by the individual as a giving-up of the self, but as a temporary relinquishment of one kind of self-interest in favor of fulfillment of another kind.

Compromise of this sort is difficult for individuals who had to comply with demands and expectations regardless of their own needs. These individuals experience relinquishing self-interest as a one-way street, rather than a temporary and compensatory detour. For example, if a child is expected to be constantly pleasant and well-mannered regardless of his or her real emotional and physical needs, being polite becomes a coercion rather than a compromise. If more reasonable expectations were made of the child and he or she could be polite or impolite and still be certain of being loved, then the child could choose to be polite and not feel coerced into being so.

The consequences of such childhood dilemmas, where true self has been sacrificed in order to maintain crucial relationships, are evident in Anaïs's published, unedited adult diaries, which reveal her battles with depression, her struggle for a sense of identity as a woman and a writer, and her perceived need to maintain secrecy and lies in her intimate relationships. In the following excerpt from *Incest, A Journal of Love*, Anaïs describes her efforts to reconnect with an authentic sense of self. She wrote this entry after an appointment with her psychiatrist, Otto Rank:

January 20, 1934
   I seduced the world with a sorrow-laden face and a sorrow-laden book. And now I am preparing to abandon this sorrow. I am coming out of the cave of my own protective books. I come out without my book. I stand without crutches. Without my great, dissolving pity for others, in which I saw deflected the shadows of an even

greater self-pity. I no longer give pity, which means I no longer need to receive it.

I think of a self-portrait tonight in order to disengage my self from dissolution. But I am not interested in it, or perhaps my self is beyond resuscitation. I am spent, wasted, lost, given, empty.[11]

As an adult, Anaïs's numerous, simultaneous sexual relationships and the secrecy and lies necessary to maintain them have been both lionized and ridiculed. These behaviors, however, are also the legacy of her childhood and are evidence of the difficulty she had developing and maintaining authentic intimacy. An example of her need for deception and the necessity for duality in her relationships can be observed in a diary entry from March of 1932. She had just returned home after a liaison with Henry Miller and was waiting for her husband, Hugo to return:

The truth is that this is the only way I can live: in two directions. I need two lives. I am two beings. When I return to Hugo in the evening, to the peace and warmth of the house, I return with a deep contentment, as if this were the only condition for me. I bring home to Hugo a whole woman, freed of all "possessed" fevers, cured of the poison of restlessness and curiosity which used to threaten our marriage, cured through action. Our love lives, because I live. I sustain and feed it. I am loyal to it, in my own way, which cannot be his way. If he ever reads these lines, he must believe me. I am writing calmly, lucidly while waiting for him to come home, as one waits for the chosen lover, the eternal one.[12]

Though Anaïs appears to accept the need for deception, she rationalizes her behavior to herself, anticipating how hurt Hugo would be if he found out. Anaïs often remarked that she needed numerous partners because she could not be all of herself with any one individual, but the compulsive quality of her multiple relationships indicates more of a pathological symptom than an expression of free will.

Anaïs's multiple relationships include the one with her diaries. From the time she first began them, she was compelled to write in them, except for two brief periods. One was in compliance with her analyst, Otto Rank, and the other was towards the end of her life. She also could not, without great struggle, transform the activities and characters in her diaries into fiction, a situation that often tormented her. The reasons for these compulsions provide us with insights about how her diaries functioned for her psychologically. To create, it is necessary to be able to play unselfconsciously with ideas, to be able to lose the self temporarily. To do so without fear, however, it is first necessary to have a reliable and authentic self to which to return. Because Anaïs did not have uninhibited access to this true self, both her relationships and her creativity were obstructed. Her diary-writing was as much of an analgesic as a source of creative expression.

The following excerpt from *Linotte* illustrates Anaïs's early exploration of her identity vis à vis her family. It is dated May 20, 1915, when she was twelve years old. Her mention of her father's arrival is a wish she keeps alive, for Joaquin had made no plans nor promises to come to the States, and Anaïs had not seen him since he walked out two years earlier:

May 20, 1915

I forgot (I blame it on my occupations) I forgot to buy a notebook in which I could reunite with my diary, so I am writing on this sheet of paper and shall insert it in my notebook.

I have never taken the trouble to make a portrait of myself for my diary. It's fun to talk to someone without saying who one is. Now I think I shall perform that little duty.

I am Angela Anaïs Juana Antolina Rosa Edelmira Nin y Culmell. I am twelve years old at present. I am rather tall for my age, everyone says. I am thin. I have large feet and large hands with fingers that often are clenched from nervousness. My face is very pale and I have big brown eyes that are vague and that I am afraid reveal my crazy thoughts. My mouth is big. I have a funny laugh, a passably nice smile. When I am angry, my mouth becomes an ugly pout. Usually I am serious and somewhat distracted. My nose is a bit the Culmell nose, by which I mean it is a little long, like Grandmother's. I have chestnut hair, not very light in color, which falls a little below the shoulder. Maman calls them locks of hair. I have always hidden them, either in a braid or tied back with a hair ribbon.

My disposition: I get angry easily. I can't stand to be teased, but I like a little to tease others. I like to work. I adore my mother and father and above all my aunts and all the rest of the family, not counting Maman, Papa, Thorvald and Joaquinito. I love Grandmother. I am crazy about reading, and writing is a passion with me. I believe fervently in God and in everything that God tells me through His holy Church. Prayer is something to which I have always had recourse. I don't love easily and become attached only to people whom I respect in my own way. I am a French girl who loves, admires, and respects her country, a real French girl. I admire Spain, although less, of course, and I especially admire Belgium.

My diary knows my thoughts as well as I know them myself. I have finished my portrait now, because a very sweet magnet has just attracted a kiss from Maman for me, and with the dream of Papa's arrival I am going to sleep after this day of work.[13]

Though given to hyperbole and romantic self inflation, Anaïs nevertheless demonstrates an ability for reflection, a need to understand herself and her environment, and an already important relationship with her diary. The mention of her father's imagined arrival indicates her efforts to ward off the painful reality that he is not coming back. *Linotte* is full of these kinds of entries, in which hyperbolized recitations often belie Anaïs's depression and helplessness. Anaïs's diary entries of August 13th and August 14th, 1914, shortly after her arrival in New York, offer an example of her efforts to defeat the chronic depression that frequently threatened her well-being:

August 13, 1914

Description of heaven on earth. Green lawns strewn with flowers, tiny houses, little white roads neatly designed, a few trees, bright sunshine, small gardens full of flowers. My Aunt Edelmira's house is arranged in exquisite taste, white furniture, everything is small, nice, very clean and orderly. A swing, bicycles, a nice little girl cousin, a friendly boy cousin, a good kind aunt whom no one could help loving. I have to say hurrah for Kew Gardens, hurrah for the house, hurrah for my aunt, hurrah for the flowers and the fields, hurrah for God who has sent us to this earthly Paradise.

August 14, 1914

…I forgot to say that last night my aunt gave a party for the grownups and Maman sang a tonadilla. I don't know why but I began to cry and cry, no doubt I thought I was back in Barcelona. I don't know myself why I cried while Maman was singing and everyone laughing.[14]

Taken out of context, the first entry appears to be the enthusiastic, exaggerated response of a young girl's thrill as she discovers a new country and a new home. The second entry, however, illuminates the first as a desperate attempt to fight against a sense of helplessness and depression that is not yet fully understood. Another example of this type of effort to change reality through idealization appears in the following entry from April 30th, 1915:

I have just finished reading 'Les Grandes Tristesses

d'Alice.' It was beautiful. A proud rebellious girl, an
orphan for two years, is sheltered by an uncle. Things
look dark, she is always serious, always in a bad frame of
mind. Her uncle is very unhappy, and so is his brother,
his sister-in-law, his friends. One day Alice runs away
and hides behind a bush to weep over what she terms
the world's wickedness toward her. She overhears a
conversation between her cousin Henri and her brother
Robert. Poor girl, growing up without her mother,
and without anyone to tell her she has the wrong idea...
The name 'Mother' had never been mentioned, but
now Alice promises herself to do better and to change
her thoughts. That sweet word brought her to herself
and she becomes cheerful and obliging. Her uncle is
very happy and everyone is pleased when Henri asks for
Alice's hand in marriage. She accepts, for it was he who
invoked her mother, is he who made her happy and
will continue to do so. This story is full of sadness,
painful separations and death, so I was moved in spite
of myself, and Alice makes me think that more than
ever I should listen to darling Maman's counsels. While
I have her I should love her always and in return God
will keep her for me always.[15]

In this excerpt, it is more obvious that Anaïs is warding
off her own fears of abandonment and loss, and trying to
protect and reassure herself of the continuity and safety of
her relationship with her mother.

Throughout *Linotte*, Anaïs expresses her struggle with
depression in the conflict she experiences between reality

and dreams, a theme that she continued to explore as an adult. The following journal entries express her sense of isolation and alienation and the dream world to which she resorts to soothe herself:

November 24, 1915

... Don't dream of happiness any more, but struggle with reality. That is my cry, but there is no echo. I want to dream, and my soul is torn between dreaming and living. Which is better? I am going to think about it.

... In New York, lonely as I am, I have reflected, I have understood, and it was here I knew the hand of misfortune that weighed on me, without understanding why. Life can no longer have any charm for me and I think that dreams, which so far have helped me to live, will be my only guide. And in moments of the deepest distress, I close my eyes and go to faraway lands where nothing can trouble the happy life that, so it seems, carries me to the other side.[16]

October 26, 1916

In the book 'The Song of the Bells,' I found my idea of a heroine in all her beauty and naïveté. Yes, that's how I imagine a little spirit who is always near me and whispers in my ear: 'To dream is to live, to live is to dream.'

And I dream ... and I dream ....[17]

April 14, 1916

[Referring to a school exam]

Those are the only little incidents which come along from time to time to trouble a little bit more the stormy waters of my life.

In the life that I lead in the infinite, it's different.

There, all is happiness and sweetness, since it is a dream.

There, there is no school with dark classrooms, but there is God.

There, there is no empty chair in the family circle; it is always complete.

There, there is no noise, but the solitude that gives peace.

There, there are no tears, for it is a smile.

That is the infinity where I live, for I live twice.[18]

Though Anaïs began her first diary at a time when one might expect a precocious adolescent to start one, her early childhood trauma and her intense, lifelong relationship with her diary set this journal apart from most adolescent diaries. Usually, they are made redundant by the real relationships that eventually replace them. Though Anaïs did not suffer from a lack of relationships, her diary, by her own admission, was her most reliable confidante.

It is, of course, impossible to say how, or even whether Anaïs might have utilized her journals if she had had an accepting, healthy parent or other adult to whom she could relate during her adolescence — someone who could understand and openly admire her and her hopes and goals. She did not. Instead, she made use of her journals as a tool of creative expression and transformation and often as a means to cope with intolerable thoughts and feelings. They provided emotional safety at the cost of creative growth.

Anaïs frequently resorted to omnipotent self-idealization to protect herself from helplessness and depression. In a journal entry of August 1919, when she was sixteen, she describes how a lie to her mother was necessary and enabled her to alleviate her mother's stress and fatigue. It also gave Anaïs a sense of competence and some degree of control:

> And when Maman comes home tired from New York, with her head full of the worries and fusses at 158 West 75 where everybody argues, when she reaches her clean little cottage and sits down to dinner while the three children and I entertain her with long meandering stories about how brave and smart Joaquinito is, how much Thorvald helped me, and even if she knows that Joaquinito probably didn't behave too well and Thorvald wasn't a great help, those happy fibs can only do her good.[19]

The conscious purpose of Anaïs's lie to her mother was to protect Rosa from further fatigue and frustration after a difficult day. The unconscious purpose was not only the containment of Anaïs's own anxiety about both her mother's well-being and her own, but also the alleviation of her feelings of guilt and responsibility for her mother's exhaustion. Only three months after this entry, Rosa suffered a nervous collapse.

The following excerpt was written in November of 1915 when Anaïs was twelve years old, struggling to come to terms with her parents' separation:

> ... I admire the classic author who wrote, honor above all. I hate modern laws which allow divorce and allow homes to be destroyed. And it seems to me that if I had a man as master, I would be submissive and, even if he deceived me, I think that I would never love another, never. And it seems to me that if I had to divorce, I would rather die, because I think it is dishonorable. Oh! How can one love a person one time and another time come to hate him? Myself, I have only one heart, only one promise, only one answer, and once a deed is done, I would never go against it.[20]

This excerpt expresses, in all its fervent poignancy, Anaïs's efforts to deal with the profound confusion and loss caused by her parents' separation. She creates through the use of words that have the significance of vows, a reality designed to keep her safe from loss no matter what the future may present. By stating her position on marriage and fidelity with such concrete certainty, Anaïs is attempting to make her beliefs facts, thus protecting herself from events that are out of her control and have the potential to cause her emotional harm. It is ironic that in her later life, she was compelled to have multiple, simultaneous, secretive relationships that were a defense against her fear of loss and rejection and the difficulty in achieving true intimacy.

In another passage, Anaïs refers to her depression as her "unbearable disposition," an appellation adopted from her mother, and one with which Anaïs felt obligated to comply:

> May 25, 1916
> I become more and more sad. My disposition is unbearable and today I have felt like crying more than six times because Maman scolds me, Thorvald runs away from me, and Joaquinito makes fun of me. I am ashamed, I am angry with myself, but impatience continues to rule my heart, my actions, my mind and my tongue. Ah! I am so unhappy to be like this![21]

Anaïs clearly takes on her mother's reproaches and locates within herself the source of her own unhappiness.

The following two excerpts from 1920, written one day apart, a few weeks before Anaïs's seventeenth birthday, demonstrate her struggle to banish her helplessness and create an ideal scenario out of the reality of her very real depression and disappointment. In the first example, Anaïs expresses her depression and her anxiety about her mother's impending month-long trip to Cuba. Implicit in this segment are Anaïs's fears of loss and rejection, and her helplessness in the face of her mother's temporary abandonment. The next day, she tries to undo her dread, through idealization of her relationship with her mother and fantasies about her boyfriend, Marcus:

> February 4, 1920
> ... Oh! I think that Maman's departure is going to be a

horrible despair! In the midst of everything I do, her absence is my predominating thought. Then I shall be poorer than the beggar dying of hunger and cold on a winter night, poorer than the poorest of the poor, deprived of sun, light, air — Life — without Maman! I know that if ever her absence went on longer than 4 weeks, 4 months, 4 years, I would die of sorrow. There now, I am crying. All alone in my Nest, my eyes full of tears. Where does so much weakness come from? The Little Flower seems to understand and comfort me.

February 5, 1920

... Fortunately Maman has delayed her trip until Sunday evening. She has her head full of numbers, my little mother does! I found out today that she is forty-eight years old. I thought she was at the most thirty-eight! I have never seen so much vitality, energy, courage and beauty combined as they are in her!

Perhaps one of the things that I love the most in Maman is that she is always mocking me. For instance, today I was telling her that when I try to be funny, I become sarcastic, and Maman said that I spend my life like a tragedienne. She didn't want to explain that statement and I have to be content with trying not to think any more about it, but I would really like to know what I am. One day I wrote that I thought the home of Romance is the moon, which shows how far away I thought it was. And I still haven't changed my mind. For me it's simple to reach the moon and look at my cherished dream, but sometimes, oh! dearest diary, I think that I am unworthy of loving and being loved! Prince Marcus is mistaken, but how can I destroy his dream of idealization when I know how attached a poet is to his dreams! Oh, just as I would suffer if he were not what I think he is!

A tragedienne, yes, an actress — if I make people think that I am good. How can I present myself before the public without a disguise, since they wouldn't recognize me like that![22]

The idea of disguise, of compliance with others' expectations, describes the dynamic by which Anaïs is attempting, above all, to make herself lovable. It is a defensive abdication of loyalty to the self in the hopes that loyalty or compliance with the other will protect her from her own self criticism and feelings of unlovability. By denying her depression and the conflicts in her relationships, she is able to imagine an idealized, perfect self she feels she must be to be loved.

When she feels in danger of losing her mother, because of Rosa's impending trip to Cuba, Anaïs idealizes her mother's mockery, which she often experiences as painful and, in the process, perfects her mother, their relationship, and her own character. She seduces a compliant, lovable, daughter-self into the place that was previously occupied by a frightened, depressed, and angry self. When she fears being unworthy of Marcus's love, she does the same with him, idealizing him by referring to him as "Prince" Marcus and making the decision to attempt to be what he wants and needs her to be in order to please him and maintain his affection for her.

Both of these examples communicate the desire for control that is implicit in the act of seduction. Anaïs attempts to create a particular kind of desired self so she can control or maintain other people's love for her. With the help of her journals, Anaïs attempted to seduce into being a self that was lovable beyond reproach.

Throughout *Linotte*, Anaïs also makes references to the need to be understood. The themes of being understood that first appear in *Linotte*, are sometimes expressed by the image of a mirror as a reflection of the self — a metaphor that fascinated Anaïs throughout her life. Her early thoughts on the metaphor of mirrors, or mirroring, and their relationship to her self-development appear in a diary entry of April 14th, 1916, when she was thirteen years old and looking for a reflection of herself in her instructor, Sister Gertrude:

> April 14, 1916
>
> At last. I have taken up my pen again. In my earthly life, nothing is changed. I am doing good work in school, and I have learned a lot from my teacher, Sister Gertrude, whom I already like a lot. Her moody and rather fussy disposition commands my attention. I study all her actions as though I were looking in a mirror, because except for the religious order, Sister Gertrude's personality is exactly how I shall be when I am grown up.[23]

This excerpt describes Anaïs's efforts to know herself, to identify traits in someone else that might help her recognize and understand her own character.

In a reference to her diary as a mirror, a reflection that captures her essence and makes it real and meaningful, Anaïs writes on March 16th, 1916, just after her thirteenth birthday:

During these days, I have let myself get carried away with writing fairy tales, but I had difficulty describing the wonderland where my mind was. I traveled to that faraway land where nothing is impossible. Yesterday I came back, to reality, to sadness. I am making fun of myself and I don't want to go on with my stories, which I called Stories of a Mirror. Now that foolishness is past. I have broken my mirror and it is silent. I am only afraid that one fine day the longing for that wonderland may take hold of me again and then my magic mirror will speak. Why? Because I have a mirror! My diary. Isn't it a mirror that will retell to oblivion the true story of a dreamer who, a long, long time ago, went through life the way one reads a book? Once the book is closed, the reader can go on his way with all the treasures it had to teach.[24]

Anaïs is writing here about her wish to be seen by a future, unknown reader. She is also describing an important dynamic function of her diary: to transform her life experience from trauma to treasure.

A more mundane reference appears on June 5th, 1919, when she is sixteen years old, studying her reflection in a mirror and finding herself wanting:

I am writing because I have a few moments. I am already dressed. I have on my pretty blue dress, white shoes,

and stockings, a coral necklace, my hair is in a chignon
with curls, and to complete my ensemble I have a pretty
bouquet of pink carnations that Emilia sent me. But
more than ever, when I look at myself in the mirror, I
think I look sad because I'm not pretty, and sometimes
I would really like to be pretty.[25]

It is noteworthy that the few times Anaïs did feel understood
by others, she experienced tremendous relief and took up her
journal with a vital and uninhibited quality that communicates
her sense of self-acceptance and connection with another.
The following is a description of an evening she spent with
her mother's friend, Mrs. Sarlabous:

January 18th, 1917
[a month before Anaïs's 14th birthday]
    I gave her [Mrs. Sarlabous] my opinion of certain
books. We both admire Shakespeare, almost all of whose
works I know by heart. After that, since I found in Mrs.
Sarlabous the first person who understands a great many
of my ideas and impressions, I talked to her about my
diary, my tastes, my thoughts in general, my opinions,
my impressions and everything.

When I saw that she understood me and approved, I
could hardly contain my joy. I told her that I like legends
better than anything. She then said to me: "But you like
legends because you have a poetic soul, my dear child!"
Ah, it pleased me so much to hear that! I admitted to
her that I dislike New York, that I find it cold. And

while I talked, I couldn't help casting an admiring glance at the beautiful books. Their colored bindings and titles printed in gold made me want to own them all. Mrs. Sarlabous followed my glance, and to my great pleasure, she rose and opened the big bookcases and showed me several books.

Well, to tell the truth, I have never revealed so much of that world of dream, thoughts and impressions to anyone as I did to Mrs. Sarlabous. I felt like dancing with joy, for I saw that she didn't make fun of me, she didn't say, as Maman does, "Now you are being dramatic!" with that mocking accent and tone that almost everyone uses with me when I say just a few words. I saw that I was saying thousands of words to Mrs. Sarlabous and that she was not mocking.[26]

There are significant correlations between the emerging self of Anaïs's childhood diary and the woman and artist into whom she later developed. The emerging self of the young Anaïs Nin that evolves over the six years of *Linotte* is a sensitive, intelligent, creative, and depressed young woman who is attempting to maintain her sense of self and her relationships with her mother and father through idealization and the maintenance of an idealized fantasy life when emotional pain becomes too great. Her fear of abandonment and her chronic anxiety regarding trust, dependence, and security in relationships are also evident. She defends against potential loss primarily by complying with her early experiences of abandonment, abuse, and neglect, and by taking full responsibility for maintaining the love and affection of people whom she loves and admires. In *Linotte*, we first see the blurring between reality and fantasy that Anaïs struggled with throughout her life, as when she defends against depression through denial or idealization. In the later diaries this conflict becomes even more evident, when, upon preparing manuscripts for publication, Anaïs edited out and/or rewrote entire episodes, intentionally presenting them as accurate representations of her original experiences.

Themes of loss, separation, betrayal, and self-perfection remained important throughout Anaïs's life. Until the end of her life, Anaïs enacted her early abuse and the loss of her father in almost all her intimate relationships. She worked hard to present to her reading audience — through editing, rewriting, and deletions — an idealized version of herself. The coquette in *Linotte*, the natural flirt who revels in the attention of as many boys as possible, prefigures the sexually compulsive adult Anaïs. Although some feminists have applauded Anaïs's sexual adventures as an exercise of freedom, it is quite clear, given what is now known about her history, that she was more driven by trauma and unconscious conflict than by sexual desire as expressed in the freedom to choose and enjoy numerous sexual partners and adventures.

The organizing principle of Anaïs Nin's life as a child was the belief that she was burdensome, profoundly ugly, and unlovable, and that if she could make herself beautiful and lovable, she could win her father back and reunite her family. Her father's abandonment and her mother's constant criticism and inability to protect her, which Anaïs experienced as proof of her lack of worth, were the dominant experiences that formed her concept of herself, and against which she fought throughout her life. The need to prove herself worthy of being loved became a compulsion to seduce, and it was not resolved until the last years of her life.

Linotte was begun as an innocent, conscious seduction. The role of seduction in Anaïs's life continued to develop and did so less innocently over time. Its role became even more complicated when she was in her early thirties and engaged in a sexual affair with her father, hoping that the actual consummation of their relationship would finally enable her to feel loved and whole.

This concrete, incestuous expression of filial devotion only deepened Anaïs's confusion about her own relational needs as well as intensifying her disappointment in her father. Her childhood attempt to seduce him from his life of selfish indolence and irresponsibility cannot be separated from her attempt to discover/create/seduce into being a self she could experience as worthy of love and attention. This idealized self-creation was also a symbolic rejection of her mother, and caused Anaïs much guilt as she attempted to disidentify with the woman her father had left.

As a child, Anaïs's inability to mourn the loss of her father kept him psychically near. It was as though she experienced him as a missing piece of herself, an essential enzyme without which she could not digest life or continue to grow. Anaïs's continued efforts to lure her father back into her life were attempts to assert her own power in the face of total helplessness. As long as she could try to create a lovable enough self to win him back, she could maintain hope in her eventual lovability while protecting herself from the truth of her father's malignant narcissism and lack of regard for her.

Linotte is a dramatic expression of the strivings of an exceptionally creative, intelligent, and sensitive young girl and her efforts — sometimes successful, sometimes not — to make sense of a traumatic and disappointing world:

> November 23, 1916
>
> Sometimes I feel as though I am forty years old because I think I have already suffered so much. I am ashamed of myself when I let myself dream of happiness, because I know, I understand that I deserve only misfortune, yet how much I have suffered and still suffer when evening comes. I have only one true friend left and that is my diary, which forces me to understand part of myself.[27]

One of the most striking features about Anaïs that we first see in her childhood diary and that also characterizes the entire body of her work, is her insistent effort to deal creatively with loss and disappointment. The physical and emotional brutalities she endured as a child were not well understood or appreciated by those from whom she sought help as an adult. The psychological establishment of the time was of little help, nor was the patriarchal culture into which Anaïs was born. Needless to say, in such a climate, Anaïs received little understanding. Nor did she garner much support for promoting a flourishing self whose artistic strivings would not be in conflict with her desire for relationships.

Anaïs made the following statement at a graduation address in 1976, a year before her death:

> By beginning a diary, I was already conceding that
> life would be more bearable if I looked at it as an
> adventure and a tale. I was telling myself the story of
> a life, and this transmutes into adventure the things
> which can shatter you.[28]

Because there has been so much conflict about Anaïs's
life and work, it is especially important to make an effort
to understand her as a whole person, much in the same way
that as clinicians, we seek to understand our patients, not as
collections of symptoms, but as whole people responding to
their environments and struggling to make meaningful lives.
My initial motivation in writing this book was to understand
more fully a woman whom I deeply loved, who influenced
my life and work, and who offered me the support and
encouragement of which she was deprived. As I wrote, I
realized that I was also motivated to provide for others who
are interested in Anaïs, a means by which to analyze and
interpret her history and the way it influenced her. As we
know, behavior does not necessarily express what it appears
to express. To attempt to know someone solely by his or her
actions is similar to appraising a home by walking around it
and evaluating its appearance. Until the foundation, wiring,
plumbing, roof, etc., are inspected it is impossible to determine
whether or not the building's appealing facade truly represents
its structural integrity or if, perhaps, it is only a superficial
distraction from crucial flaws.

If an analysis is a portrait of a life, it is a portrait that is
created and interpreted, not merely captured and observed.
A good photographic portrait is one that freezes a moment

in time, and in so doing expresses or evokes some essence of its subject that adds to the picture a third dimension: meaning. An analysis culls factual moments and passes these events through the lens of understanding in an effort to make meaning of the events and experiences that are the artifacts of human existence. My goal has been to present a thorough and compassionate investigation of the many influences that contributed to making Anaïs Nin who she was. As she herself said, "... the destructive element of truth is neutralized" [by a] "deep probing" [of] "motivation: What is understood is not judged."[29]

To take her comment a step further, what is understood is almost necessarily loved, because understanding cannot exist without empathy, empathy without compassion, and compassion without love.

Notes: Part III – Understanding Anaïs

1. Winnicott, D.W., 1971c, pp. 54-55.
2. Nin, A., 1978, p. 400.
3. Bair, D., 1995, p. 100.
4. Webster, M. (Ed.), 1960, p. 765.
5. Nin, A., 1978, p. 39.
6. Evans, 1981, p. 976.
7. Nin, A., 1978, p. 10.
8. Nin, A., 1966, p. 11.
9. Ibid., p. 242.
10. Nin, A., 1978, pp. 143-144.
11. Nin, A., 1992, p. 302.
12. Nin, A., 1986, p. 60.
13. Nin, A., 1978, pp. 65-66.
14. Ibid., pp. 14-15.
15. Ibid., p. 61.
16. Ibid., pp. 95-96.
17. Ibid., p. 142.
18. Ibid., p. 117.
19. Ibid., p. 298.
20. Ibid., pp. 90-91.
21. Ibid., p. 124.
22. Ibid., pp. 432-433.
23. Nin, A., 1978, p. 116.
24. Ibid., p. 109.
25. Ibid., p. 241.
26. Ibid., pp. 153-154.

27. Nin, A., 1978, p. 144.
28. Ibid., p. vii.
29. Fitch, N. R., 1993, p. 415.

PART IV

⤳

AFTER ANAÏS

⤳ When a camera is tightly focused on one detail of a scene so that detail fills the entire frame, perception of the whole is obliterated and even the detail may appear as an unidentifiable abstraction. A clinical study of a friend or loved one is similar in its propensity to distort because studying discrete details of a person's life inevitably obscures the whole person.

The process is similar to looking at figure-ground cards developed to test visual perception. Depending on whether the viewer is attending to the dark or light part of the visual field, a very different picture emerges. Focusing on the light area of one of the cards reveals a goblet, while fixing on the dark part discloses two silhouetted faces, and vice versa. What is most compelling about studying these cards is how focus and perception can create experience, how quickly perception can change through a fluctuation of focus, and how inseparable any object of study is from its surroundings.

This psychological study of Anaïs is vulnerable to the same kinds of distortions — of not seeing the forest for the trees — because it necessarily focused on her problems and the etiology of her behavior. Writing this book, I was concerned at times that I would lose track of Anaïs and begin to see her as a collection of symptoms. Fortunately, this has not been the case, and in fact, through understanding her psychology, a more fully human and authentic woman has emerged.

The Anaïs I knew when I was a young woman and the Anaïs I discovered since her death are no longer contradictory. They have been integrated into one: a woman who made time for friends, who was loyal, unselfconsciously generous, funny, and a fine cook, as well as a woman who had a need to lie, deceive, and hide. Embarking on a clinical study of Anaïs has brought together her seemingly disparate selves.

Often, I wonder what Anaïs would think of who I have become. Everything she wanted for me has come to pass: work I am eager to go to each day, friends who are truly family, the love of a spouse who knows all of who I am and still is delighted to come home to me. And all of this has happened in just the way she anticipated: through joy, loss, pain, hard work, generosity and love from numerous people, and, I attest, good fortune. I have found my way, though I am aware that the journey is not yet over.

I did not know all of Anaïs at the time of her death, but I knew her and loved her. In the intervening years, I have learned a great deal more about her secrets and the part of her she tried to conceal. In Autumn of 1939, anticipating World War II, and reflecting on her own life Anaïs wrote, "When you live closely to individual dramas you marvel that we do not have continuous war, knowing what nightmares human beings conceal, what secret obsessions and hidden cruelties" (Nin, A., 1967, p. 346.).

You also marvel at the courage, capacity for love, and creativity of which human beings are capable in spite of the monsters lurking within. Witnessing the hidden, painful truths Anaïs concealed allowed all who knew her and those who will come to know her through her work, to understand and value her more completely.

Since her death, Anaïs has visited me many times in dreams. Most recently, we sat before her hearth in Silver Lake and she asked me not to publish this book, warning me that I would be exposing myself to criticism and misunderstanding. I awoke anxious for myself, but mostly fearing that publication somehow would be a betrayal of her. Then I remembered the dream she had had before the first volume of her diary was published, in which she opened her front door and was met by a nuclear explosion. She feared publication of her diary would wreak destruction not only on herself, but on others she loved, just as I fear publication of my book might discredit me or somehow harm her memory. It was an act of bravery for Anaïs to have published her diaries. Many readers, myself included, have benefitted because she did. It is her courage that made this book possible.

If time were malleable I would arrange to tell Anaïs just one more thing: she had nothing to hide. Knowing her, flaws visible, makes her more lovable, not less.

This book is a gesture of gratitude to Anaïs Nin — to all she was and was not.

PART V

⌒

DEAR DIARY

FURTHER THOUGHTS ON
DIARY-KEEPING & THEORY

⌒ The portrait I have presented of Anaïs Nin is necessarily skewed. Though it is based on her diaries and two biographies, the information garnered from these sources has been filtered through the subjective lens of my relationship with her. I have constructed a portrait of Anaïs by exploring and analyzing her inner life and connecting the dots between the child she was and the woman she became. In much the same way, I strive to understand and help my patients, piecing together their histories and experience to form a three-dimensional portrait of their lives.

In formulating the "case" of Anaïs Nin, I considered her chaotic, violent childhood, early and serious illnesses, abuse and rejection by a sadistic, seductive father, guilt about and responsibility for an unhappy mother. I also examined the ways she defended herself against the helplessness and fear these developmental insults caused: self-blame, idealization of her parents, and an attempt to fashion a false identity to win their approval and love.

While informed by psychological theory, I avoided a highly abstract theoretical discussion to stay as close as possible to Anaïs's experience. When I have made theoretical forays into the nature of child development and its pathology, my aim was to illuminate a particular aspect of Anaïs's experience or behavior. In this sense my analysis of Anaïs is complete.

There are, however, ways to pull back the analytic lens, broadening the unit of study to highlight more abstract issues in order to clarify not what is unique in Anaïs's experience, but what is universal. The lens of choice in this endeavor is that of British psychoanalyst, D. W. Winnicott. The focus of analysis is the nature of creativity and the psychological functions of diary-writing. After all, Anaïs probably spent more time with her diaries than with any one person. Though the content of her journals has shed light on much of her inner life, what about the form itself? Why do people write diaries? What functions do they serve? Understanding the functions of creative expression as related to diary-writing in general will provide further insight into this diarist in particular.

Before applying Winnicott's ideas to the psychological functions of diary-writing, a short history and description of the phenomenon are necessary to establish a general context in which to think about the specifics of Anaïs's life, creativity, and relationship to her diary.

A History of Diary-Keeping

⌣⇢ The words "diary" and "journal" are used interchangeably. Both have their roots in Latin — diary from *dies*, or day, and journal from *diurnalis*, also meaning day — thus defining the purpose of diary-writing as the creation of a record of the experiences of each day. The earliest record of diary-keeping dates to tenth century Japan. Women of the royal court kept "pillow books," which were personal records of daily thoughts and reflections. Entries were diverse and ranged from concerns about family relationships and health matters to meditations about religion and politics.

Robert Fothergill studied the history of diary-writing in Great Britain and was interested in the development of diary use as a form of personal expression. He noted the importance of travel diaries of the 17th century in which thoughtful observation was important to accurately record and communicate the dangers and delights of the unknown world. Because travelers at that time were crucial sources of information, these early diaries were of necessity an interface between public and private space, the personal/psychological use inseparable from the public/social use.

The diaries of travelers can be compared with those that focused exclusively on spiritual and moral self-examination in the service of self-improvement, such as the journals of conscience employed by the Puritans and Quakers. The primary purpose of these journals was to examine and control, if not exorcize, unwanted impulses such as greed, envy, lust, and selfishness.

Towards the end of the 18th century and into the 19th century, however, a transition from the laundry list of sins and improvements metamorphosized into "recording things you may need to remember," which in turn transformed into "recording things you want to remember." [1] This is the precursor of what is commonly accepted as the modern diary. About this current form, Fothergill notes, "the wish to remember seems to be associated with the wish to be remembered," [2] implying a relationship with a real or imagined other who will eventually read the diary. Because the diarist now had an imaginary future reader, a bias was naturally introduced. The diary was to be bequeathed to posterity and it behooved its author to present him or herself in an optimal light. It is easy to see how Anaïs expressed this bias to an extreme degree.

There is also a distinction between diary development in 17th, 18th, and 19th century Europe and Great Britain, and diary development in the United States during these centuries. For American pioneers, the diary was an essential instrument of communication and support. Because of the geographical distances that separated people and the slowness and unreliability of mail service in the new world, these early diaries took the form of continuous autobiography. They were created to record events that might later be shared with others in the service of community-building around common experience. Because early pioneers were frequently exposed to potential physical dangers, their diaries also served as personal histories for relatives and friends should the diarist meet an untimely demise. As well as helping their authors maintain continuity and integrate new experiences, pioneer diaries imply potential readership, communication, and preservation of self and community.

PSYCHOLOGICAL USES OF DIARY WRITING

A diary, as compared to an autobiography, has a sense of emotional immediacy because it is both about the writer's life and it is also part of the writer's life. The diary is a statement of being, and the process of writing in the diary is an act of being, creating a relationship between writer and diary similar to the relationship that exists between artists and their work. As a repository and creation of facts, fantasies, hopes, fears, and dreams, the diary becomes both a process (the act of writing), and a form (the notebook, paper, ink, computer screen, etc.) The immediacy and continuity of journal-writing define the diary as a perennial work in progress that can provide the diarist with an ongoing sense of self. The diary need never be mourned because it need never be finished, and in fact, may outlive the diarist, as is the case with Anaïs.

This quality of perpetuity can infuse the diary and the diarist with the illusion of immortality. Both the diary and the process of writing it ward off and acknowledge the diarist's mortality, for the diary will only be finished upon the diarist's death. Given this, it is easy to see how a diary might provide its author with a sense of control in the face of environmental trauma, or loss and disappointment in relationships. In this sense, diaries express a type of omnipotence. The ways in which diarists employ their journals are an interface between external reality and internal psychological experience.

DYNAMIC CATEGORIES

An important contribution to the study of journal use is Thomas Mallon's 1984 investigation, *A Book of One's Own*. Mallon informally classifies seven psychological categories of diary-keeping according to patterns he observed after reading numerous journals. Though Mallon's categories are theme-oriented rather than theoretical, they are dynamic in nature and focus on the primary psychological use expressed in each category. Overall, they provide an informal but useful and beneficial structure that can be applied to the shifting relationships that Anaïs had with her diaries, often simultaneously using them for multiple psychological functions and seamlessly shifting among multiple categories and uses.

Mallon classifies diarists according to the following seven groups based on the primary dynamic function of the diary to its author: 1) Chroniclers, 2) Travelers, 3) Pilgrims, 4) Creators, 5) Confessors, 6) Apologists, and 7) Prisoners.

CHRONICLERS

Mallon describes chroniclers as those who experience the need to record and review the details of daily life. They make use of the diary, "... as carrier of the private, the everyday, the intriguing, the sordid, the sublime, the boring—in short, a chronicle of everything." [3]

The root of the word, chronicle, is chronos, or time, specifically the passage of time, expressing the psychological motivation of chroniclers, "to hold on to it all, to cheat the clock and death ..." [4]

This category emphasizes how loss and the passage of time contribute to the need to keep a diary, symbolically preserving what the writer considers precious.

Given this definition, Anaïs's diaries certainly have attributes that would include her among the chroniclers. The loss of her culture, extended family, father, and social standing, and the psychological impact these losses had on her identity formation were certainly motivation enough to impel her to figure out a way in which she might preserve the things and people she held dear. The act of chronicling her life enabled her to name and hold on to experiences that might otherwise have been lost and to deal with feelings that threatened her growing sense of identity and development.

TRAVELERS

Traveler diaries record the experiences of their authors as they move geographically outside the context of their familiar culture, family, home, and relationships. One of the functions of a travel diary is to help its author integrate new experiences. The travel diary serves an important bridging function. It can be used to make meaning of trauma such as cultural dislocation, during which an identity that has been taken for granted may be challenged, new experiences incorporated, and the concept of self eventually reconfigured. The travel diary can connect the unknown and the familiar, functioning as an internal gyroscope as it helps the traveler adapt to new cultural paradigms. The category of traveler clearly includes Anaïs, who often had to adjust to new expectations and cultural assumptions. In fact, a primary motivation for beginning *Linotte* was to help her work through these changes and attempt to come to terms with being uprooted and displaced.

PILGRIMS

〜 Pilgrims are those who keep journals in the service of discovering and/or creating their true selves. Mallon explicitly identifies May Sarton, Henry David Thoreau, and Anaïs as examples of this genre of diarist. One of the major features of pilgrim diarists is their obsessive relationship to their journals and the absolute insistence of following a personal inner path. As the name implies, pilgrims have a spiritual relationship with their diaries, and make use of them as tools for discovering, exploring, and creating their true natures.

CREATORS

〜 For creators, the next category Mallon explores, the diary is employed to "... sketch and brainstorm, private pages on which invention's audacity can fly or fail, where the words and shapes and rhythms and systems that educate humankind's sense and imagination can first come to life." [5]

This category describes an uninhibited experience that enriches the individual and promotes the pleasure of creativity for its own sake. Mallon includes in this category writers, artists, and any diarists who keep a journal primarily for the pleasure of playing with ideas and words regardless of their eventual application.

One of Anaïs's conflicts throughout her life was her struggle to use her diary in just such a way. It was difficult, if not impossible for Anaïs to use the diary in a playful or symbolic fashion that might have helped her to write fiction. She was trapped by the concrete facts and actual emotions of her life and often had trouble converting them to the symbolic, metaphoric fiction that she so avidly wished to create. In a journal entry of May 22, 1919, when she was sixteen years old, she describes her struggle to both create fiction and write in her journal, lamenting that she is not able simultaneously to manage both:

May 22, 1919

I would never have believed that ideas could really move out, just like ordinary furniture, but it has happened. The reason was simply that they didn't have enough room and they were jostling around in my head in a manner that didn't please me. So I took a big sheet of paper, pen and ink, and I wrote a long time, arranging my ideas carefully on that big blank page. In that way my ideas slowly emerged from the disorder and found themselves, with pleasure, in the light of day. When they had all come out, in the form of the beginning of a book, I was satisfied and could throw myself again into the tasks that preoccupied me before.

During all that time, I wrote only a few words here [in the journal], because the kind of ideas that were troubling me were not the kind that I usually write in this notebook. It was impossible for me to write both things at once.[6]

As an adult, Anaïs often separated the contents of her journals and the contents of her fiction, consigning tolerable thoughts and feelings to the journal, and split off, unacceptable aspects of herself to her fiction. She explained that she felt she could only record certain feelings and events in the form of fiction because she was afraid she might otherwise cause unbearable pain to those she loved. As Noel Riley-Fitch notes, writing of Anaïs's life between 1923 and 1927:

> Her turn to fiction results from a fear of dealing with explicit issues in her diary. The anxiety over her conjugal failure, her feelings about Eduardo, and her attraction to other men are secrets best placed in fictional form rather than in the confessional of her diary. A veiled reference to a 'subject' that she has long wanted to write about but cannot because it will create 'trouble' certainly refers to sex.[7]

An example of this split is the erotic story "Lilith," which deals with the early, sexually naïve years of Anaïs's marriage to Hugo. "Lilith," which was written in the early 1940s and published after Anaïs's death in 1977 as part of the collection *Delta of Venus*, is the fictionalized, but more accurate version of a young couple's inexperience and difficulty in consummating their marriage and exploring their sexual yearnings.

Confessors

～ The next category, the confessional journal is one that is written specifically, consciously or unconsciously, with the reader in mind. As psychologist Susan Boxer explains:

> Here the diarist carefully guards his privacy so as to express forbidden wishes and deeds, which is a means of realizing them in symbolic form; the excitement for the writer is immensely enhanced by the fantasy of being found out. The reader, as the object of these confessions, is seduced, drawn-in, and tantalized. Cast as judge, absolver, voyeur, he is an integral part of this drama, present in the diarist's mind and written into the script long before he arrives on the scene.[8]

Mallon says of the confessional diary, "The secrecy, this conspiracy, is what animates the confessional diary beyond all others."[9] At the same time that secrecy is paramount, the diarist is simultaneously imagining an audience. It is clear that the confessional diary is a crucial category, if not the principal form of Anaïs's journals.

Apologists

～ The apologist diary, like the confessional diary, is another example of writing with a specific audience in mind. Unlike the confessional, however, which emphasizes self-criticism and self-reproach, apologists argue for their experience and point of view as valid and correct. Like confessors, apologists write for a current or future reader with the intention of shaping or controlling the reader's good opinion of them. Anaïs also belongs to this category, for though she frequently reproaches herself, she also directly and indirectly argues for her point of view. For example, at age twelve, Anaïs describes her faith in God:

May 12, 1915

God put us in this world to make us hate sin. All of us humans are weak and we are dazzled by a brilliant light full of reflections that weigh on us too late. We are dazzled, I say, and instead of realizing that the world is laden with sin and vices, we admire it and have chosen it as our mother. Horror and remorse which forever seize us too late, poor blind ones that we are! God has granted me infinite grace, He has allowed me to see a tiny light which revealed the vice, the horror that encumbers the world. He has explained to me the sweetness that His heart holds and I have understood; thus I have given myself completely to that divine heart. I am full of pity for the blind ones. I am full of gratitude toward God.[10]

PRISONERS

Prisoners are those diarists who for one reason or another, cannot live in the real world, and whose relationships with their diaries become substitutes for experiences and relationships that are unattainable in real life. The prisoner diary is a world of wishes that belongs to "... the imprisoned, the frightened, and the slowly dying."[11]

Because of the effort to overcome uncontrollable circumstances, these diaries are inspirational rather than depressing because they demonstrate courage and determination in the face of overwhelming odds. Mallon states "... for these people, diaries are not simply habits; they are attempts to create life, and if they sometimes fail, they retain the luster of heroism." [12]

During the last year of her life, when she wrote the journal entitled, *Book of Music*, Anaïs could be categorized as a prisoner. She created this journal to help her cope with terrible physical pain by focusing on the transformational qualities of the music her husband, Rupert's string quartet played at their home and that she listened to on a regular basis during the process of dying.

DEVELOPMENTAL FUNCTIONS
OF THE ADOLESCENT DIARY

In writing about adolescent diarists, Peter Blos emphasized the dynamic functions of journal-writing that facilitate the developmental tasks of this particular period in which a transition from childhood dependence to adult independence and identity integration is in progress. Referring to this transitional period as the "second separation individuation,"[13] Blos emphasized the developmental push for a greater integration of ego functions as well as the capacity to tolerate the opposing emotions associated with staying connected to important others while striving for differentiation:

The need to keep a diary is inversely proportionate to the opportunity the adolescent has of sharing freely with the environment his emotional urgencies. Daydreams, events, and emotions which cannot be shared with real people are confessed with relief to the diary. The diary thus assumes an object-like quality.[14]

If, as Blos suggests, the need to keep a diary is inversely proportionate to the adolescent's opportunity to share his or her authentic self with real people in the environment, Anaïs's need to keep a journal must have been terribly acute. Throughout *Linotte*, Anaïs observes the necessity of keeping her thoughts and feelings to herself, lest she burden or contaminate others. For example, in May of 1915, at the age of twelve she writes, "... I am a bundle of illnesses that should be thrown out for fear they may be catching. But I close up my bundle and no one catches anything."[15]

This excerpt demonstrates the way in which Anaïs assumes both full responsibility for her painful feelings and the despairing assumption that sharing these feelings could not comfort her. She maintains a strong prohibition against expressing her authentic experience to anyone but herself and her diary. On January 17, 1915, shortly before her twelfth birthday, she writes:

Only my heart can explain how I feel, my pen cannot do it. Perhaps my feelings are absurd, I think so and I shall stop. All that makes me feel like crying and I contain myself only with great difficulty. I can't explain this state of mind. Luckily I manage to conceal it and no one sees or guesses. If I suffer, I mustn't make the others suffer too. Besides, what good would it do? Would their sorrow help console me for mine: No, so only my diary has the right to suffer like me, to think like me, since its destiny is to hold my heart's most secret thoughts.[16]

In describing the dynamic functions of the adolescent journal, Blos emphasized the developmentally facilitating aspects of journal-writing, including the maintenance of important relationships, the grounding of mental activities and fantasy life in reality, limiting sexual acting out, facilitating the ego functions of mastery and synthesis, and promoting a greater awareness of internal life. His emphasis was on the use of journal writing as a non-traumatic facilitator of natural development that has not been complicated by trauma.

DEFENSIVE-ADAPTIVE USE OF THE ADOLESCENT JOURNAL

In contrast to Blos, Katherine Dalsimer, in her study of the *Diary of Anne Frank*, emphasized another function of adolescent journal-writing, which is that of relationship replacement or substitution. It is important to note that the subject of her study, Anne Frank, was the victim of unusual historical circumstances. The typical age-appropriate adolescent tasks Frank was encountering were eclipsed by the hideous reality of her precarious situation. Though Anaïs was not subject to such an extreme of socially sanctioned persecution, she too, began her journal at a time of relationship loss and social dislocation that added a degree of complexity to the already difficult developmental tasks that adolescents are expected to master. Anaïs's adolescent journal was forged out of the press of severe emotional stressors, and it often possesses more the quality of an action taken for symptom relief than as an enhancement to promote a difficult, though normal, developmental push.

Using Anne Frank's diary as the basis of her investigation, Dalsimer focused on the function of the diary as a safe relationship, more or less under the omnipotent control of the writer, and thus a pliable recipient of the diarist's thoughts and feelings. In this way, Dalsimer stressed the diary's function as something to be called upon specifically during times of separation or loss that contains and represents a relationship undergoing change:

> It is a unique form of communication in which one has only to speak and never to listen. It is a literary mode whose legitimate subject is the self. It reflects the fluidity of self-esteem in adolescence — the alternation between self-disparagement and self-aggrandizement — that the diary is valued both because it will guard one's shameful secrets and also because it may one day be published.[17]

Focusing on the developmental struggle of the adolescent move from childhood to adulthood, Dalsimer emphasizes the journal's function as a means of preserving the past — not just past events, but the internal experience of these events. Dalsimer describes the diary's primary function as relational in that it creates an understanding and available other who is able to provide the diarist with the emotional closeness that cannot be found among the actual people in the diarist's life. The diary is a confidante who "... allows the adolescent to take hold of what would otherwise be fleeting, transitory states, to capture something of the inner life and make it permanent."[18]

This is particularly true in situations in which the writer is experiencing some kind of trauma or relational loss and is able to make use of the journal to help in mourning and integrating such experiences.

Dalsimer also points out how the adolescent diary maintains the writer's connection to past relationships by recreating the state of merger experienced in the infant-mother unit, while at the same time asserting the adolescent's separateness by its very creation and the secrecy in which it is written and maintained, "The diary does not assert the separateness by seeing things differently than the writer does. The fiction is fervently maintained that the diary is another person ... like the mother of infancy who is continuous with the self." [19]

The developmental properties of the diary may change, however, if a situation of loss, abuse, or trauma is particularly acute or becomes chronic. When this occurs, the journal can begin to take on concrete, magical qualities as the young diarist struggles to deal with internal pressures in a non-supportive environment.

The psychological meaning of diary-keeping for each individual diarist sheds light on the relationship between writer and diary. Exploration of these meanings furthers our understanding of Anaïs and of art in general, because diary-keeping is a form of art, a creative and expressive activity that has both a private and a public meaning. It is private in that a diary is usually a highly personal act of self-expression. It is public in that it has a real or imagined audience, the formal qualities of language and narrative, and is a product that is experienced as outside the self.

Even a casual review of some of the theories about diary-writing includes references to psychoanalytic theories that explore the function of such writing during the developmental phase of adolescence. According to traditional psychoanalytic theory, the diary functions as a confidante, allowing the adolescent to maintain important relationships during the phase of separation from his or her parents. The diary is a tool with which the adolescent writes about, and thus manages, anxiety provoking sexual and aggressive impulses that are gradually surfacing. It represents the adolescent's claim to have an inner life independent of the parent, but avoids any overt rupture of these vital ties.

In situations in which there is little communication between parent and child, the diary may even substitute for these relationships, giving the adolescent a feeling of being seen and understood. Whether in psychological health or illness, these theories tend to understand diary-writing as an adaptive attempt at mastery during a phase of life in which turbulent feelings are emerging and complicating the normal process of separation and individuation.

THE OBJECT RELATIONS THEORY OF D.W. WINNICOTT

There is another theory that explains human development, psychopathology and emotional health, and also offers a comprehensive way to think about the psychological functions of diary-writing, general creativity, and Anaïs's particular relationships to these phenomena. This is the object relations theory of psychoanalyst D.W. Winnicott, a British pediatrician turned psychotherapist whose writings in the 1950s and 1960s on the mother-child relationship marked an important change in psychoanalytic thinking.

The term object relations refers to the centrality of the interpersonal relationships that are formed in the early years of life and establish how we later interact with others, particularly those with whom we are emotionally intimate. In this context, the word "object" refers to a person. Winnicott was particularly interested in how a mother-infant relationship in which the infant is psychologically merged with and totally dependent on the mother, evolves into a relationship in which the child functions independently and recognizes his or her own and the mother's unique, separate subjectivity.

Prior to Winnicott, traditional psychoanalytic theories viewed the infant as a bundle of impulses barely aware of the surrounding world. In Freud's view, the problem for the child was how to develop a sense of reality when all he or she wanted was to gratify impulses. According to Freud, reality stood in opposition to the infant's need for instant gratification. It was endured rather than actively sought, and relationships were considered a means to an end instead of a primary need in and of themselves.

The tradition to which Winnicott adhered, British object relations theory, disagreed with Freud. Object relations theory argued that infants developed and thrived by adapting to reality, sought relationships for their own sake, and were fundamentally social creatures, not merely need-satisfying ones. Winnicott took this idea a step further, proposing that the most important developmental issue was the fact of the infant's complete dependence on the mother and therefore, it was impossible to understand an infant's inner life without also considering the mother's care. To understand human psychology, Winnicott theorized, the mother-infant dyad should be the primary unit of study.

Winnicott was one of the first clinicians/theoreticians to challenge the psychoanalytic assumption that the infant experiences him or herself as a separate, differentiated person. His greatest contributions to clinical treatment and psychoanalytic theory explore the question of how the newborn, wholly dependent upon his or her mother for survival, develops into a simultaneously differentiated and relational being.

Winnicott stands out among object relations theorists in that he was one of the first to emphasize the importance of the actual relationship between the mother and her growing child, rather than focusing on the infant's unconscious representation of this relationship. Though Winnicott accepted the precepts of psychoanalysis and the influence of the unconscious, he believed it was the actual relationship of the real baby to his or her real mother, and the baby's actual dependence on that real mother, that determined the developing child's unconscious processes. This emphasis and understanding were informed by his work and observations as a pediatrician — a role in which he was called upon to heal pre-verbal patients suffering from such illnesses as feeding disorders and autism. He remained prominent in pediatrics throughout his work as a psychoanalyst.

Most of Winnicott's clinical and theoretical writings were fashioned as oral presentations to clinicians and laypersons, particularly mothers, and as such, they possess an informal, discursive quality that invites query and interpretation. The emphasis on paradox and dialectic that is the hallmark of Winnicott's ideas is implicit in his style of thinking and writing. His language tends to be poetic, dramatic, and experiential as he describes the importance of dialectics and paradox in human development. As Stephen Greenberg and Jay Mitchell describe:

> Almost all his contributions center around what he depicts as the continually hazardous struggle of the self for an individuated existence which at the same time allows for intimate contact with others. Winnicott's depiction of the healthy self rests upon one of his many paradoxes — through separation, nothing is lost, but rather something is gained and preserved: "This is the place that I have set out to examine, the separation that is not a separation but a form of union."[20]

Because Winnicott insisted upon the acceptance of unresolved paradox and the primacy of real relationships and experience, and because his style paralleled the paradoxical content he expressed, it is as difficult to paraphrase his ideas and preserve their original impact as it would be to describe a particular piece of music to an audience who has not heard it. In thinking about Winnicott, it is helpful to remember the multidimensional and experiential quality of his work — the counterpoint of multiple, related themes in constant, fluctuating relationship to each other, similar to the relationship between the pianist's right and left hands as he or she plays the bass and treble clefs of a piano concerto.

Winnicott's writings are grounded in clinical observation and practice, full of metaphor, paradox, and the necessity of tolerating important contradictions without resolving them, just as even the best relationship must contain necessary irritations as well as satisfactions. Winnicott's approach to psychological development provides a context that explains how the textures and nuances of actual relationships form a template for the dual task of understanding and promoting psychological health and understanding and treating psychopathology.

For purposes of clarity, the following discussion will be presented in diachronic form, stage by stage, through the maturational process. This structure has evolved out of a distillation of all of Winnicott's individual papers, which emphasize the paradoxical, synchronic, experiential processes of maturation. The linear structure presented here is imposed for the sole purpose of making discussion and application of Winnicott's work more manageable.

CREATIVITY

It is not of course that anyone will ever be able to explain the creative impulse, and it is unlikely that anyone would ever want to do so; but the link can be made, and usefully made, between creative living and living itself, and the reasons can be studied why it is that creative living can be lost and why the individual's feeling that life is real or meaningful can disappear. [21]

— D.W. Winnicott

⌒ The above quotation could have been written specifically about Anaïs's struggle to understand the factors that inhibited her creative expression — factors that often resulted in feelings of meaninglessness that she attempted to combat and master in her fiction, in relationships, and in the pages of her journal.

Primary to Winnicott's thinking is the assertion that creativity has an essential place as an ongoing process in human development and daily human life. To Winnicott, creativity is the individual's capacity for spontaneous interaction between the subjective experience of internal reality and the objectively perceived facts of external reality. To some extent, this interaction always occurs, but creativity within this interaction depends upon the relative degree to which spontaneous, responsive subjectivity is present. As simple as this may sound, its achievement relies on the rather complicated relationship of appropriate maternal adaptation to the maturational needs of the ever-changing infant.

Keeping in mind Winnicott's assumption of the primacy of relationships, the natural creativity he identifies is the motivation for development, and may be seen as a logical extension of procreativity itself. When the sexual union creates a new life, that life first exists in the context of a physical relationship in which it is literally dependent upon its mother's body for nine months. In this way, the infant's first relationship comes into being before the fact of its physical birth, while it shares its mother's blood, nutrients, and physical and emotional experiences. At the time of birth, though it now has the physiological capacity to survive outside the mother's body, the newborn is completely physically and psychologically dependent upon the mother (or primary caretaker) for attentive nurturing and protection.

SUBJECTIVE OBJECT

〜 Winnicott refers to the initial postbirth phase of the infant-mother relationship as the subjective object phase, meaning that the baby (subject), perceives the mother (object), to be continuous with the self. During this period, the infant experiences the mother and the self as one being, or being one. If all goes well, the mother is able to intuit her infant's needs and meet them unobtrusively, allowing the infant the illusion that need does not exist. Winnicott used the term "primary maternal preoccupation"[22] to describe what he felt to be the mother's necessary initial identification with, and adaptation to her new baby. He argued that this preoccupation was essential in order for the mother to adapt successfully to the infant's subjectively changing needs, thus providing an appropriate facilitating environment to promote and sustain the child's healthy development:

> The environment does not make the infant grow, nor does it determine the direction of growth. The environment, when good enough, facilitates the maturational process. For this to happen the environmental provision in an extremely subtle manner adapts itself to the changing needs arising out of the fact of maturation. Such subtle adaptation to changing need can only be given by a person, and one who has for the time being no other preoccupation, and who is "identified with the infant"

so that the infant's needs are sensed and met, as by a natural process.[23]

In other words, the mother provides the baby with what it needs in synchronicity with the child's experience of the need. In this way the child experiences "... an overlap between what the mother supplies and what the child might conceive of." [24]

For example, a mother who is well attuned to her infant's needs will be able to respond to her baby's first hungry whimperings by providing the breast or bottle. When the hunger is so quickly followed by feeding, the baby perceives itself to have omnipotently satisfied its hunger simply because the need and its satisfaction were virtually simultaneous. This illusion is possible because "... the adaptive mother presents an object or a manipulation that meets the baby's needs, and so the baby *begins to need just that which the mother presents. In this way the baby comes to feel confident in being able to create objects and to create the actual world.*" [25]

It is not difficult to imagine how a child who does not have such continuity of experience, or who suffered severe illness at an early age, as Anaïs did, will have difficulty developing this kind of confidence and sense of well-being.

THE FACILITATING ENVIRONMENT AND GOING-ON-BEING

Winnicott refered to the satisfactory care of the infant by a good-enough mother — a mother who is imperfect but reliably competent — as the facilitating environment. The facilitating environment, which the infant experiences to include both the mother and the environment she provides, protects the infant from physical and psychological impingements in his or her experience of self and allows for what Winnicott refers to as "going-on-being." [26] The experience of going-on-being is essential for the development of an authentic sense of self because before one can do, one must be able to be. A baby must first have a sense of his or her own innate qualities and be able to identify and explore them before being called upon to use them. Otherwise, it is not clear to the infant if the requested response is in his or her repertoire, or if it is being demanded whether or not it is currently available.

Perhaps this unconscious dynamic of infancy is more clearly identifiable when compared to a similar, but conscious dynamic that is frequently seen in adolescents who are struggling with the developmental task of separation. In this context it is known as lying. For instance, in order to placate an anxious parent who is concerned about unfinished homework or a purloined beer, many teenagers, motivated by a desire to remain simultaneously connected to their parents, to assert independence, and to avoid conflict, may simply offer the parent the desired reassurance and hope to avoid discovery. Though the developmental tasks of teenagers and infants are very different, an infant whose sense of going-on-being is disrupted may feel forced similarly to lie, though in this case the exclusive motivation is to remain connected to the care-taker upon whom the infant is totally dependent, and the lie is an unconscious reaction to a disruption of going-on-being. Here, the infant lies by adjusting his or her reactions to meet environmental expectations even if it means overriding his or her own authentic responses. If impingements and/or neglected needs chronically disrupt the infant's sense of going-on-being, they eventually cause trauma and actual damage to the emerging self. For example, a poorly attuned mother may repeatedly change her baby's diaper long after the baby's discomfort has become pain, or may repeatedly insist on a smile from the baby when the mother herself is depressed and needs cheering up. When such situations become chronic, environmental demands are being made of the baby to respond to the mother's needs before the baby has an authentic self with which to make responses.

It is important to note that failure of the facilitating environment is very different from the necessity of relational frustration, which promotes healthy maturation and development. The difference between failure of the facilitating environment and developmental frustration is that the first is based in either neglect and/or impingement, and the second is an important component of relational development and promotion of the emerging self. It is a necessary transition between the phase of the subjective object and the phase of the objectively perceived object.

Developmental frustration occurs after the period of primary maternal preoccupation, when the good-enough mother and her infant settle into a comfortable routine. At some point, the mother again experiences needs of her own that are not perfectly attuned to those of her child. For example, because she is caught up in a book she is writing, she may allow her baby to cry for a few moments longer than usual, hoping the child will fall asleep. If the infant has had a reliable enough environment prior to such perceived failures in attunement, two maturational processes start to emerge simultaneously. The first is that the baby begins to internalize the caretaking function of the mother when she is absent during short periods of need. The second is that the infant begins to be aware that infant and mother are not a single unit after all. These two processes continue to develop through the phase of transitional phenomena. They are both produced by and inform the infant's adjustment to the gradual knowledge that the mother is outside the purview of the infant's omnipotent control.

Anaïs's tremendous capacity for empathy, intuition, and attunement can be understood in the context of childhood impingement. Her early illnesses and her mother's emotional stress interfered with her sense of going-on-being, calling upon her to interact with her environment without sufficient emotional and cognitive resources. This in turn contributed to Anaïs's extreme sensitivity to her environment, motivated by her need to intuit quickly what was expected of her in an effort to provide it and assure a safe connection with those she needed and loved. Anaïs's early impingements also provide information regarding her intermittent, life-long struggle with depression. If a child has not been sufficiently able to internalize the soothing functions of the primary caretaker, he or she will be more vulnerable to environmental assaults and disappointments because the resources to manage them have not adequately been developed.

TRANSITIONAL PHENOMENA

The phase of transitional phenomena begins when the infant is able to perceive and tolerate a greater sense of differentiation between the self and the caregiver. It is the period between the phase of the subjective object and the phase of the objectively perceived object. It is important to note that Winnicott did not relegate transitional phenomena to only one developmental period. Because transitional phenomena comprise many activities, they occur in various forms in all stages of healthy development, and, once relinquished may also recur, in primitive or pathological forms under environmental stress or trauma. Winnicott describes transitional phenomena in relation to their facilitation of interpersonal relationships:

> The transitional phenomena represent the early stages of the use of illusion, without which there is no meaning for the human being in the idea of a relationship with an object that is perceived by others as external to that being. [27]

THE TRANSITIONAL OBJECT

A hallmark of the phase of transitional phenomena is the baby's creation/discovery of the transitional object, which parallels and is informed by the child's experience of the mother as being both under his or her omnipotent control and part of the external environment. The transitional object is the baby's first "not me" [28] possession. It is a symbol of connection to and separation from the primary caregiver. Its creation/discovery occurs at a time when the child is being introduced to external reality through the process of gradual separations from the mother. Often the transitional object is soft and cuddly, such as a teddy bear, blanket, or piece of clothing, though this is not an essential requirement. Whereas the baby chooses the transitional object for its inherent physical attributes, its meaning is created by the baby because of the symbolic maternal qualities with which the baby imbues it. Thus, the transitional object has the unique and paradoxical properties of being both created and found. It is a thing the child discovers in the environment, but it has meaning because it is a creation of the child's. Winnicott emphasized the importance of the paradoxical and dialectical nature of the transitional object:

> Of the transitional object it can be said that it is a matter of agreement between us and the baby that we will never ask the question: "Did you conceive of this or was it presented to you from without?" The important point is that no decision on this point is expected. The question is not to be formulated.[29]

The creation/discovery of the transitional object normally begins sometime between two to twelve months. It is usually given up between four to seven years of age, not out of defense, but because it gradually loses its meaning to the child and is replaced by other experiences in the realm of transitional phenomena. These experiences include the use of language, playing with other children, involvement in sports, making art or music, and other activities that are "... spread out over the whole intermediate territory between 'inner reality' and 'the external world as perceived by two persons in common,' that is to say, over the whole cultural field."[30]

Anaïs's transitional object was a doll named Bouby that her father gave her and that she carried with her until her marriage.[31] The fact that her chosen transitional object was given to her by her father and her attachment to it was so prolonged suggests that it did not fully serve her developmental needs. Her constant need for the actual doll indicates an understandable lack of trust and continuity in her relationship with her father and the absence of a soothing presence to mediate her anxiety. In a healthy scenario, the transitional object helps the child begin the management of the lifetime task of maintaining the dialectic between inner and outer reality by keeping them separate but related through illusion.

ILLUSION

The use of illusion occupies an important position among Winnicott's ideas and is present in all stages of development from the phase of the subjective object, through transitional phenomena, to the phase of the objectively perceived object. During the subjective object phase, illusion allows the infant to experience him or herself and the good-enough mother as one, the infant-mother unit. This in turn promotes a relatively anxiety-free environment in which the baby may experience going-on-being. In the phase of transitional phenomena, illusion is an intermediary between reality and omnipotent fantasy. It is the baby's first use of symbolic communication through the creation/discovery of the transitional object that the child employs both to stand for and deny maternal separation.

In this way, illusion facilitates and promotes various developmental tasks by allowing a gradual interface between internal, subjective reality and external, objective reality. As Winnicott clarifies:

> I am here staking a claim for an intermediate state between a baby's inability and his growing ability to recognize and accept reality. This intermediate state is potential space, which is another hallmark of transitional phenomena.[32]

POTENTIAL SPACE

The illusory, intermediate state known as potential space first comes into being as a dynamic between infant and mother. It is a state in which the mother is no longer experienced as being under the baby's omnipotent control, but neither is she yet experienced as entirely separate and external. Potential space is that realm in which separation and unity with the mother exist simultaneously. It is usually associated with various expressions of symbolic play between mother and infant. Commenting on Winnicott's ideas about illusion and potential space, psychoanalyst, Thomas Ogden writes:

> Potential space is the general term Winnicott used to refer to an intermediate area of experiencing that lies between fantasy and reality. Specific forms of potential space

include the play space, the area of the transitional object and phenomena, the analytic space, the area of cultural experience, and the area of creativity.[33]

It is not at all a place, as its appellation implies, but a dialectical experience that both joins and separates the infant and the mother. This dialectic is a dynamic process, never static, by which mother and infant initiate and influence communication with each other. Being able to occupy potential space is essential for the development of true subjectivity and authentic self experience.

Potential space may be thought of as part of the continuum of going-on-being. In her discussion of transitional phenomena, psychologist Vivian Dent describes the mediating dynamic of potential space and its "... bridging function that simultaneously unites and separates illusion and reality without forcing firm distinctions between them." [34]

Because potential space both separates and connects self and other, it is through this phenomenon that the self is both informed by and informs the other. Like all interpersonal phenomena, the results of these interactions impact the participants according to the degree of attunement each of them experiences. If the mother's response is reliably attuned to the infant's reality, it promotes the development of the infant's true self. If, however, the mother's response is not reliably attuned, the infant will adapt accordingly, pushing his or her true response aside and inadvertently facilitating the development of a false self in an attempt to connect with the mother by conforming to the mother's needs and expectations of the infant.

To illustrate this dynamic, imagine a vital, happy, baby, being rocked in the arms of a mother who is chronically unable to attune herself to her child's moods and responses. This emphasis is important because occasional and necessary failures of attunement do not traumatize a baby and interfere with development. It is when these incongruities are the norm that the child must adjust in a distorted and inauthentic manner.

So, our imagined baby squeals with delight as it succeeds in getting an elusive toe into its mouth. The baby looks into its mother's eyes for confirmation of the thrilling deed. The mother, preoccupied with concerns about money, or the demands of her job, partner, health, etc., gazes back at her child from the confines of her concerns and worries. She does not truly see her baby's excitement, nor does she respond with matching and appropriate delight. From the infant's point of view, he or she sees anxiety, perhaps depression in the mother's eyes, feels it in her arms. As the child adjusts to synchronize with the mother's feeling state, it becomes less and less clear to the infant who is excited and who is depressed. The smile disappears from the baby's lips and the happy gurgling stops. The baby adjusts his or her emotions to match the mother's in order to feel once again connected to and part of this essential other. After repeated incidents of this sort of lack of attunement, the mismatching of mother to infant is expected by the infant, and his or her own authentic response becomes less important than connecting to the mother. In fact, the infant's authentic responses also become less accessible because they do not serve the infant in the goal of achieving maternal contact. Instead of experiencing and expressing his or her own feelings, the baby learns, through observation and intuition, to conform to the mother's mood lest he or she be alienated and isolated from the most important person in the world. Communication is obstructed and travels mainly in one direction — from mother to infant. The infant-mother unit, with its primary emphasis on the infant has been reversed and has become the mother-infant unit, in which the emphasis has shifted to the mother as the infant adapts to implicit and explicit communication from her.

It is not difficult to imagine how Anaïs might have adopted just such a response. From her history we know that she was gravely ill, which added to her mother's stress in dealing with a selfish, abusive husband, and also introduced Anaïs to an unpredictable world in which she suffered physical pain. It is particularly crucial in times of stress for a child to feel safely connected to the primary caregiver. If the mother is overly anxious and lacks adequate support for herself, as Rosa surely did, the emotional resources available for her child will inevitably be compromised.

The Psychopathology of Transitional Space and Transitional Object/Fetish Object Development

Just as the dialectic of potential space is an experiential phenomenon, a continuum that cannot be confined to precise time frames or actions, so does the transitional object/fetish object exist on a continuum that is dependent upon the fluctuations of an individual's internal resources as the individual deals with the realities of his or her environmental situation.

The transformation from transitional object to fetish object is a product of what Ogden described as the "psychopathology of potential space."[35] When external reality becomes too traumatic, impinges too forcefully, and overwhelms an individual's internal resources for coping and maintaining a meaningful exchange between internal experience and external phenomena, potential space breaks down and the individual resorts to defensive maneuvers in order to preserve any meaningful experience of self. It is within potential space that symbols first originate, illusion (internal experience over which one has omnipotent control) and reality (external experience over which one does not have omnipotent control) coexist and influence one another, true imagination blossoms, and new experiences are created and integrated. In the absence of potential space, there can be only fantasy, in which the capacity for symbolic meaning is defensively closed down. In this situation, the transitional object, a meaningful symbol, ceases to function symbolically and bridge the potential space between illusion and reality, internal and external experience. The transitional object no longer represents relationships, thoughts, and feelings, but becomes defensively concretized, one-dimensional, and inflexible in the service of protecting the individual from particular thoughts and associated feelings and providing the illusion of omnipotent control. The transitional object has become a fetish object.

A transitional object such as a teddy bear, or Anaïs's doll, can become a fetish object if the child's relationship with the mother or other important person is traumatically interrupted, for instance, by abuse, death, or abandonment. In a situation of this kind, the teddy bear or doll may become for the traumatized and bereft child a way to deny permanent absence or chronic abuse, to prevent the knowledge of this truth, rather than serving as a symbolic representation of the acceptance that the important relationship exists outside of the child's omnipotent control. In contrast to a transitional object (which need not be mourned because it gradually and naturally is relinquished) a fetish object becomes overvalued, is not internally integrated, and must be concretely and repetitively available. Therefore, it paradoxically feels more susceptible to being actually lost.

The collapse of potential space that curtails the integration of subjective and objective experience is often a result of environmental impingement in infancy, but severe fluctuations and traumatic environmental assaults during any phase of life can distort potential space and motivate a defensive foreclosure of its functions. Ogden described in detail the breakdown of potential space, delineating its causes and four possible outcomes. The most severe of these is a situation in which premature, traumatic awareness of helplessness is so overwhelming and unbearable that extraordinary measures must be taken to avoid all meaning and neither illusion nor reality are created. This scenario is typical of psychotic states in which core development either never occurred or has been dramatically distorted.

Another result occurs when the dialectic between reality and illusion collapses in the direction of illusion. In this case, illusion becomes fantasy, and the distinction between fantasy and reality is blurred. An individual who experiences this kind of breakdown of potential space may insist upon a stereotyped fantasy as the reality of life. For example, such a person may spend hours doodling notes for a screenplay that will bring wealth and fame, without ever engaging in the process of writing it. The individual for whom potential space collapses in the direction of fantasy cannot use illusion and creativity to incorporate new experiences and make use of them in the real world.

In a third possible scenario, the dialectic of potential space collapses in the direction of reality. Imagination is foreclosed and the individual relies upon the quantifiable and concrete, perhaps insisting on reductionistic and mechanized structures to mediate anxiety. For example, an individual who experiences the world in this way might insist that his or her partner or lover present flowers once a week as proof of love or insist on making a month-to-month contract that states the conditions of the relationship, while being unable to receive or initiate everyday gestures of affection, such as specially prepared meals or love notes out of which continuity of relationship spontaneously evolves. The goals of these maneuvers are certainty and predictability based on rational, cognitive, contractual interactions with others in a world that is experienced to be unpredictable and emotionally dangerous.

In Ogden's final scenario, reality and illusion exist but are sequestered, preventing any meaningful dialogue between them. Instead, a kind of splitting occurs. The individual can experience only reality or only illusion, but is not able to establish a dialectic between the two. Ambivalence is curtailed, and intense mood swings may dominate as the individual careens back and forth between conflicting poles of a single experience. This is the dynamic that occurs in fetishism, when both external reality and internal experience exist for the individual, but remain separated because certain meanings must be avoided at all costs. The example cited earlier in which a teddy bear transforms from transitional object to fetish object typifies this dynamic, as does Anaïs's relationship with her doll, Bouby.

Bouby came to represent concretely Anaïs's relationship with her father in an effort to deny the reality of his abandonment and abuse. That she carried Bouby with her until her marriage underscores her continued need to defend against the painful reality of her relationship with her father. This is because illusion, being isolated and deprived of external enrichment, took on the qualities of fantasy. An individual in this state, such as Anaïs, cannot access potential creativity. The necessary and dynamic relationship between illusion and reality has been severed for the purpose of protecting the self from intolerable thoughts by separating them from subjective meaning.

Anaïs's continued, obsessive use of her diary also suggests that at times diary-writing had more of a fetishistic quality than a transitional object quality. Rather than furthering creative explorations, the diary often substituted for them, inhibiting rather than promoting her forays into transitional phenomena and foreclosing the use of illusion.

In the psychoanalytic literature, fetishes have been associated with sexual perversions, where the fetish represents a valued body part, such as a breast or penis, and simultaneously denies a forbidden thought, such as the fact that women do not have penises.[36] The origination of fetish use has been traced to the period in which genital differences between boys and girls are first perceived, usually between two to five years of age, linking fetish development in both children and adults with castration anxiety and penis envy. Because the period of perception of genital differences is concurrent with the use and acquisition of symbols, it stands to reason that a disturbance in this period may be expressed in some form of maladaptive symbol development.

Though various schools of psychological thought propose different theories regarding the etiology, use, and meaning of fetishes, all agree that fetishes are the concretization of symbols or metaphors. Given this premise, it stands to reason that the fetish develops due to some breakdown in symbolic communication where metaphor no longer suffices and only a concrete representation will do. The process by which this breakdown occurs is the result of trauma and how, under severe stress, functions of potential space, illusion, and imagination can fail to provide meaningful symbolic expression.

Though Winnicott does not specifically refer to an experiential continuum from transitional object to fetish object, his discussions on the dialectical nature of transitional phenomena and the pathology that results when the phenomena of potential space are foreclosed suggest such a continuum, as do Ogden's discussions on the pathology of transitional space. Psychoanalyst Joyce McDougall also alludes to a transitional object / fetish object continuum in her discussion of pathological transitional objects, which she calls "transitory objects."[37] She defines these as objects or experiences that exist somewhere between a transitional object and a fetish object or perversion. They can include addictions, people, substances, and sexual behaviors.

The child's environmental experience will determine whether the transitional object will be able to perform its function of helping the child make the transition between the illusory state of the subjective object and the phase of the objectively perceived object. When the growing baby's environment is good-enough, the transitional object is a bridge that both connects and separates internal and external experience. In normal development, the child gradually lets go of the transitional object. This occurs when, at his or her discretion, the child can smoothly manipulate symbols such as language to create a satisfactory inter-face between internal and external reality.

When the child's environment has been chronically or acutely traumatic, however, the transitional object may become concretized and inhibit imagination and spontaneous interface between internal and external reality. In such a situation the child is forced into reactivity, and, as psychologist Abbott Bronstein notes:

> Then, the capacity for illusion is undermined by the needs and conflicts experienced by the child. Potential space — where symbols exist, has collapsed. Now the object itself is more important than the mother. It is not a substitute for her. The infant's experience becomes like that of the fetishist — the object itself provides the comforting, soothing, and containing of his fears. A split in the ego has appeared. The infant becomes addicted to the object and suffers when it is removed. It is now a fetish.[38]

When trauma leaves the child psychically unprotected, he or she must expend a great deal of energy fending off painful, intrusive thoughts, and attempts to regulate the anxiety that such impingements produce.

In a relatively trauma-free environment, the creation/discovery of the transitional object is motivated by the natural process of maturation in the context of a facilitating environment. In this environment, the transitional object appears just as it is needed, when the baby is beginning to discover that infant and caregiver are not one. The child's use of the transitional object enables him or her to experience, express, and master ambivalent feelings about this change in self-and-other perception. Once the transition from subjective object to objectively perceived object is completed, the transitional object is no longer needed by the child. It ceases to have meaning and is naturally relinquished in favor of other explorations in potential space.

In contrast, the fetish object becomes necessary due to environmental failure. Trauma of some kind has interrupted development and the child cannot safely rely on environmental provisions, resorting to fantasy in an attempt to gain control of the uncontrollable. As Bronstein describes, "... instead of the symbolic capacity to have and use illusion, ... we are now able to define the infantile as well as the adult fetish object as the replacement for the ambivalently loved person by the omnipotently controlled fetish object." [39]

Rather than contributing to a continuing dialectic and integration of experience between illusion and reality, the fetish becomes a repetitively relied upon, concrete, external, object that impedes experiential development and integration while protecting the self from overwhelming or intolerable assault through the use of magical, omnipotent control.

An example of fetish object dynamics that can be observed in popular culture are the ways in which substances are often used and abused in the service of altering affect or mood. Though many of these substances, such as alcohol, tobacco, and heroin, have a chemically addictive component, they also serve psychological functions and can be used fetishistically. Mood-altering substances that efface or banish an unwanted psychological state paradoxically emphasize that state, for acknowledging the wish or need to alter one's mood further illuminates it, just as the shoe fetishist's high-heeled slipper both denies and insists upon the knowledge that castration is possible.

Need for Symbolic Communication

〜 Healthy initial engagement in transitional phenomena is of particular importance because it is during this period of development that the need for symbolic communication first arises. Think for a moment about the healthy infant-mother unit of the subjective object phase. Assuming that the infant has had good-enough mothering, he or she experiences self and mother as one. Need and satisfaction are simultaneously attended and there is no perception on the baby's part of foreground (self) and background (mother and the environment she provides). From the baby's point of view, there is only the omnipotent subjective self, and, therefore, no need for communication. It is only through the gradual experience of frustrated need states that the baby becomes aware of separateness, first experiences its true dependence, and must deal with the need-dependence-separation continuum. In order to do so, the baby requires symbols to communicate with this separate entity. The recognition of separateness and the resulting knowledge that one's needs must be met by an other produces a new need: the need to communicate.

COMMUNICATION AND LANGUAGE

Symbolic communication is often first expressed through the creation/discovery of the transitional object, which communicates symbolically the unchallenged paradox that "... the infant and mother are one, and the infant and mother are two." [40]

Along with the emergence of the transitional object, the infant begins to organize random sounds, and through the mutative exchange of these sounds with the mother, eventually develops a permanent sound-meaning to designate the transitional object. The child may also begin to imitate the lullaby the mother sings before bedtime, and as the melody becomes associated with the mother's presence and acquires symbolic maternal meaning, the child may begin humming it as a symbol of relatedness to the mother. In this way, language itself falls into the category of transitional phenomena.

Because language has few concrete qualities apart from sound, rhythm, and physical vibration, it is one of the most abstract and adaptive means of communication. Due to its malleability, meaning is assigned to words through the use of culturally accepted grammar and vocabulary. The qualities of language that imbue it with meaning provide the user of language with power to organize and thereby transform experience through the use of symbols.

It is also important to note the differences between spoken and written language. Speech, on the one hand, assumes a present other with whom one is communicating, while writing assumes either communication exclusively with and for the self, such as some uses of diary-writing, or with an other who is absent. Given these differences, both speech and writing could be transitional phenomena and/or transitional objects, depending upon their subjective purpose. One of the criteria that determines the transitional nature of language, spoken or written, has to do with the individual's experience of the relative contribution of internal and external reality and the intended purpose of the spoken or written word.

CAPACITY TO BE ALONE

Up to this point, assuming that the baby has had good-enough mothering, we can expect that he or she has experienced a relatively trauma-free subjective object phase, and through the use of transitional phenomena and a transitional object, has begun the paradigm shift from the infant-mother unit to the infant-and-mother dyad. The next development we may expect to observe in the baby is also paradoxical in nature, directly related to emotional maturity, and includes the emergence of a reliable, spontaneous sense of self that is capable of the experience of shared external reality. According to Winnicott, this development is the capacity of the child to be alone.[41] Its paradoxical nature is based in the fact that in order to be alone, the child must first be able to be alone in the presence of someone else, usually the primary caregiver.

The reason that the capacity to be alone is so important is that it rests upon the premise that the child has been able to internalize a good-enough relationship and that this good relationship is in the process of being integrated into the child's psychic reality and self-experience. In order to achieve the developmental task of being alone, the child must be reasonably free from painful internalized relationships. The achievement of this developmental task also implies that the child has had a good-enough experience of going-on-being, for the capacity to be alone requires access to a relatively anxiety-free experience of self, which first develops in the dynamic of going-on-being. An example of the capacity to be alone may be seen in the scenario of a child playing contentedly with an assortment of toys while his or her mother works at the computer in another room. In this scenario, the child plays securely with no conscious thought about the protective person/environment, yet the child knows without question that the person/environment is present.

It is important to differentiate the capacity to be alone from defensive isolation, because they can look very much the same. The capacity to be alone has a relaxed quality about it and is an expression of freedom. It arises out of the dialectic between internal experience and external reality and is creative and exploratory in nature. Defensive isolation, on the other hand, is a maneuver to protect the self from some kind of threatening affect such as depression, anger, or anxiety. It is a reaction to impingements of one's sense of going-on-being rather than a response to the dialectic between internal and external environments. Whereas the capacity to be alone is dependent upon the integration of a good-enough object relationship, defensive isolation suggests the integration of a persecutory object relationship that prevents or interferes with the dialectics of potential space and signifies the presence of chronic anxiety that must be addressed or managed.

Ego Relatedness

〰 Winnicott refered to the dynamic between mother and infant that allows the infant to be alone in the presence of the mother, and later to be actually alone, as ego-relatedness.[42] The process by which this is achieved occurs naturally as the mother cares for her infant and her mature ego strength balances her infant's immature ego development. Gradually, the infant internalizes the mother's ego-supportive functions and, over time, is able to be alone without anxiety or the need for either the actual mother or a symbolized version of her. Without sufficient exposure to being alone in the presence of an other, however, the infant's ability to develop the capacity to be alone may be impaired or may not develop at all.

The reason that this developmental task is so important is because it is only in the context of anxiety-free solitude that the infant is able to discover his or her own idiosyncratic sense of self. It is in this neutral, non-demanding environment that a sense of true self and agency develops, when reference to internal reality may be trusted and relied upon, and a sense of vitality prevails.

If the capacity to be alone is hampered or does not develop at all, the consequences can be devastating. An individual who has not developed the capacity to be alone is vulnerable to impingements from the environment, one of the most problematic of which is dependence upon the environment for a sense of identity. Reliance on others for self-identity may be manifested in a number of ways, but usually involves a defensive false self organization that must continually react to external stimuli and is impaired in its ability to make and maintain authentic connection with an available and vital core identity.

OBJECTIVELY PERCEIVED OBJECT AND OBJECT USE

When the infant no longer experiences the mother as an illusionary extension of the self, and has creatively employed the transitional object to communicate and establish boundaries between inside and outside, me and not-me, the phase of the objectively perceived object commences. In this phase, the child is able to relate to the mother as a separate being whom the child does not create, but discovers. The hallmark of this phase is the change from object relatedness to object use. This paradigmatic shift solidifies the experience of self and other as separate, and thus, paradoxically enables greater potential for deeper and more satisfying connection and inter-relational experience. Extinguishing the illusion of omnipotent control of the object firmly establishes an internal locus of control. As psychologist Jessica Benjamin explains, "When the subject fails to make the transition from 'relating' to 'using,' it means that he has not been able to place the object outside himself, to distinguish it from his mental experience of omnipotent control. He can only 'use' the object when he perceives it 'as an external phenomenon, not as a projective entity' when he recognizes it 'as an entity in its own right.'"[43]

According to Winnicott, the mother's role during this transition is to be available to the child as he or she relinquishes omnipotent control via fantasized destruction of the internalized mother. It is crucial that the mother survive the child's (fantasized) destruction, during this period which, in this context, means that the mother does not retaliate. It must be understood that the destruction of the internalized fantasy mother is a maturational task that expresses the child's need to differentiate. As Benjamin describes, "The object, in fantasy is always being destroyed because in order to recognize that it survived, exists outside, it must be destroyed inside so it is clear that it is not subject to our mental control." [44]

Winnicott made the point that destruction of the internalized object does not involve anger, and if the mother is able to facilitate the child's destructive differentiation, to demonstrate survival and relationship with the child, the child stands to benefit in some important ways. Benjamin similarly states, "First, by accepting the other's independence, the child gains something that replaces control — a renewed sense of connection with the other." [45]

Because of the dynamic relationship within which the destruction/survival takes place, the child can experience a greater sense of reliability of self as well as resiliency of the relationship that will later facilitate relational constancy. Destruction of the object is a process similar to the game of peek-a-boo in which the baby eliminates the mother by covering up his or her eyes, only to be reassured that the mother has survived this expulsion from the baby's environment and is waiting with a smile when the child is ready to retrieve her.

Another benefit for the child in the evolution from object relatedness to object use has to do with furthering authenticity and true self experience. Benjamin describes this as: "One of the most important elements in feeling authentic was the recognition of an outside reality that is not one's own projection, the experience of contacting other minds." [46]

In this way, the child comes to accept the limits of his or her own omnipotence and the boundary between self and other becomes firmer. No matter how ruthlessly the child behaves, the mother endures, secure in her own life and still lovingly available to the child. As Winnicott describes:

> The subject says to the object [the mother who he imagines is under his or her omnipotent control]: "I have destroyed you," and the object (the real mother) is there to receive the communication. From now on the subject says, "Hullo, object!" "I've destroyed you." "I love you." "You have value for me because of your survival and my destruction of you." While I am loving you [the now increasingly real external mother], I am all the time destroying you" [the previously omnipotent fantasy mother]. [47]

The implication here is that an individual cannot fully experience him or herself until this can be done in the context of being separate yet connected to the other. For example, without recognition of the difference between shoreline and sea, it would be impossible to observe and experience the ebb and flow of the tide, just as it is impossible to know an other without the development of an authentic and reliable sense of self.

True Self/False Self

It is creative apperception more than anything else that makes the individual feel that life is worth living. Contrasted with this is a relationship to external reality which is one of compliance, the world and its details being recognized but only as something to be fitted in with or demanding adaptation.[48]

〜 The two brief sentences quoted above from *Playing and Reality* present the essence of Winnicott's theory of healthy development and the consequences of development that has been obstructed. When the environment of a newborn infant is able to provide well enough for the child's needs, the developing individual grows up with a reliable and authentic sense of a true self that is exhibited in experiences of innate curiosity, agency, and creativity, and which is accessible and adaptable enough to serve the changing needs and interests of the self. If a baby's environment chronically fails the child, however, by neglect, impingement, or both, and forces the child to adapt to its environment rather than the environment adapting to the child, a very different picture develops. For example, an infant who is chronically hungry will be in a constant state of arousal, if not actual physical pain. The child will not have a secure sense of well-being and must make the most of what provisions are supplied when they appear. This failure of a facilitating environment fosters what Winnicott refered to as the emergence of a false self.[49] He compassionately explained the defensive organization of the false self as a necessary maneuver by the impinged-upon infant to protect the true self from destruction — a total loss of organization of self experience that would lead to madness:

> ... where the mother cannot adapt well enough, the infant gets seduced into a compliance, and a compliant False Self reacts to environmental demands and the infant seems to accept them. Through this False Self the infant builds up a false set of relationships, and by means of introjections even attains a show of being real, so that the child may grow to be just like mother, nurse, aunt, brother, or whoever at the time dominates the scene. The False Self has one positive and very important function: to hide the True Self, which it does by compliance with environmental demands.[50]

This paragraph describes the process by which the false self evolves out of compliance with the environment. The false self necessarily lacks the spontaneity of self-experience that develops in the context of an attentive, facilitating environment.

The false self comes into being in order to protect the true self — incipient, embattled, imperilled — from any further impingement. The false self has been called into being prematurely by the need to insure a connection with a caregiver who cannot adequately attune to the child on his or her own terms, and instead, burdens the child with his or her own emotional states.

The false self necessarily is placating. A caricatured version of it can be seen in Woody Allen's movie, "Zelig". It is the story of a man, (Zelig), who instinctively adopts the physical and emotional features of anyone important to him, morphing to identify more closely with others. In this way, Zelig protects his highly private and insecure true self and maintains at least a modicum of security in his relationships.

An evocative account of environmental pressure and false self development from the imagined point of view of the baby is available from one of Winnicott's patients, a woman who had suffered from early maternal impingement and environmental failure. She described the experience and its consequences in a moving portrait that captures the physical manifestations of an environment that fosters false self organization:

> At the beginning the individual is like a bubble. If the pressure from the outside actively adapts to the pressure within, then the bubble is the significant thing, that is to say the infant's self. If, however, the environmental pressure is greater or less than the pressure within the bubble, then it is not the bubble that is important but the environment. The bubble adapts to the outside pressure.[51]

This image of the self as bubble, subject to the natural forces of physics, evokes the fragility and utter dependence of the infant who has no choice but to comply with environmental pressures or risk bursting or imploding.

Given Anaïs's history of environmental pressure and chaos, paternal abuse and absence, and physical illness, it is not difficult to understand how false self development might have served her. Because emergence of her true self was obstructed, she needed a means of maintaining connection to those upon whom she depended. When the true self is experienced as inadequate to the task, the false self emerges, providing the necessary link to others and protection for the authentic self. Though this process safeguards the true self, it also depletes it of uninhibited, spontaneous interaction with the environment. Just as someone performing guard duty must remain alert and forego relaxed appreciation of the night sky, Anaïs had to protect herself from threats of loss in her connections to those she loved. Insecurity and hypervigilance were an inheritance with which she struggled much of her life.

In contrast to the false self, the true self provides the individual with vitality and the capacity for a meaningful dialectic between internal and external worlds. The true self experiences an external reality sufficiently free from an anxious pressure to conform, as well as an internal reality sufficiently free from persecutory feelings and fantasies to enable him or her to engage creatively in the transitional area of experience and to make use of such experiences. Of the true self Winnicott says, "There is but little point in formulating a True Self idea except for the purpose of trying to understand the False Self, because it does no more than collect together the details of the experience of aliveness." [52]

It is by virtue of this comparison that we can understand important differences in how true and false self personalities experience and behave in the external world. One of the major differences between true and false self personality organizations is the ability of the true self to compromise adaptively, compared with the necessity of the false self to comply.

COMPROMISE AND COMPLIANCE:
TRUE AND FALSE SELF ENVIRONMENTAL INTERFACE

The ability for compromise is a developmental marker that is more easily identified once the rudimentary mastery of abstract reasoning and language have been attained. It is observable in the context of an individual's social and interpersonal life. The ability to compromise is predicated upon the development of a reasonably accessible true self which, in turn, is predicated upon a reasonably responsive self-environment relationship.

Compared to true self development, the individual who develops a predominantly false self organization is being asked to react to external demands that have no internal counterpart and are therefore experienced by the self as impositions or intrusions. For example, a baby who is not hungry is awakened from a nap and forced to take the breast. In this scenario, the external reality of the breast has no internal analog with which the baby can make sense of the experience. If this type of intrusion becomes chronic, the child may come to expect the external world to intrude upon his or her experience and he or she will have no alternative but to comply.

Contrast this to the experience of a baby who cries spontaneously because he or she is hungry and is then given the breast. Here, the experience contains analogous components in the infant's internal and external reality. The experience of hunger in the baby's internal reality is met by the external reality of the breast. Thus, internal and external experience begin to interface meaningfully. With experiences of this kind reliably repeated, the child comes to know external reality as benign, responsive, and complementary to internal reality, and is able effortlessly to maintain his or her experience of going-on-being and connection to true self experience.

Though Winnicott believed the ability to compromise was an important developmental benchmark, he also believed environmental compliance to be on a continuum, and held out hope that "... even in the most extreme case of compliance and the establishment of a false personality, hidden away somewhere there exists a secret life that is satisfactory because of its being creative or original to that human being. Its unsatisfactoriness must be measured in terms of its being hidden, its lack of enrichment through living experience." [53]

In comparing compromise and compliance, Winnicott saw the defensive use of compliance as a splitting from the essential creative core in which fantasy usurped imagination and the dialectic between internal and external experience was attenuated or curtailed. The distinctions between the functions of imagination and fantasy — how each serves to enhance or obstruct creativity and true self experience — are important features in the etiology of psychological health or pathology.

IMAGINATION AND FANTASY

⌒ The roles of imagination and fantasy are intimately related to Winnicott's theories of creativity and development, and specifically connected to his ideas about true and false self organization and expression. Though imagination and fantasy may share such elements as contents and intensity, their functions and etiology are quite different.

Imagination, which is a phenomenon of potential space, is the developmental result of a good-enough facilitating environment. It promotes personal enrichment and growth through a creative dialectic between internal experience and external reality. An example of how imagination functions interpersonally may be seen in the way in which a child employs a transitional object, imbuing it with particular qualities and using it in such a way that he or she can express and master experiences of attachment to and separation from the mother.

One of the salient features of imagination is spontaneity, which may also be seen in the example of the child and the transitional object. The child, without inhibition, has responded to the environment and chosen a transitional object with which he or she is able to express internal feelings such as love and anger as they arise.

Imagination originates spontaneously from within and is experienced in potential space as a response, not a reaction to the external environment. For instance, if the child is angry or frustrated because his or her mother is spending too much time at work, the child may enact this love-hate ambivalence by throwing, hitting, ignoring, or giving special care to the transitional object. Imagination functions both consciously and unconsciously. In dreaming, though repressed, imagination still operates to integrate internal experience and external reality. Even when imagination is repressed it has been integrated into the unconscious apparatus and is still available to connect and separate realms of experience, much as a bridge enveloped by fog still exists, though its structure cannot be perceived.

The ways in which imagination and transitional phenomena facilitate development are infinite. The following two examples illustrate the breakdown and repair of transitional experience, clarifying their critical importance. The first, a situation reported by Ogden, concerns a child with a phobia about taking a bath:

> A two-and-a-half-year-old child, after having been frightened by having his head go underwater while being given a bath, became highly resistant to taking a bath. Some months later, after gentle but persistent coaxing by his mother, he very reluctantly allowed himself to be placed in four inches of bath water. The child's entire body was tense; his hands were tightly clamped onto his mother's. He was not crying, but his eyes were pleadingly glued to those of his mother. One knee was locked in extension while the other was flexed in order to hold as much of himself out of the water as he could. His mother began almost immediately to try to interest him in some bath toys. He was not the least bit interested until she told him she would like some tea. At that point the tension that had been apparent in his arms, legs,

abdomen, and particularly his face, abruptly gave way to a new physical and psychological state. His knees were bent a little; his eyes surveyed the toy cups and saucers and spotted an empty shampoo bottle, which he chose to use as milk for the tea; the tension in his voice shifted from the tense insistent plea, "My not like bath, my not like bath," to a narrative of his play: "Tea not too hot, it's okay now. My blow on it for you. Tea yummy." The mother has some "tea" and asked for more. After a few minutes, the mother began to reach for the washcloth. This resulted in the child's ending of the play as abruptly as he had started it, with a return of all of the initial signs of anxiety that had preceded the play. After the mother reassured the child that she would hold him so he would not slip, she asked him if he had any more tea. He did, and playing was resumed.[54]

In the beginning, the child could not play, could not transform the medium of the bath into something his imagination could make safe. The water was just water, an unalterable fact. Because of his prior experience, it was frightening. With the help of his mother, however, the water became something that had personal symbolic meaning to the child. It became "tea." In his imagination, the child transformed the bath water to tea, and robbed it of its frightening meaning by substituting a new one. Because of his secure relationship with his mother, the boy was able to use his imagination to master a trauma. Through the use of transitional phenomena, mother and son created a new experience in which the boy was no longer helpless and in danger of slipping beneath the surface of the water. He was serving his mother the "tea" she requested and he created, restoring his capacity for transitional experience.

The second example of how transitional phenomena facilitate the mastery of trauma and support development can be found in the use to which the Norwegian painter, Edvard Munch made of his paintings. Munch is probably best known for his painting "The Scream," an iconic image of existential horror, in which a figure on a bridge, open-mouthed, distorted, stares out of a dark canvas. Munch frequently painted haunted, melancholic, frightening figures whose origins can be traced to the trauma of witnessing, at the age of five, his mother's bloody death from tuberculosis, and his sister's death ten years later.

Images of these losses led to Munch's inability to look anyone, particularly women, in the eye. He avoided gazing directly into any woman's face, fearing he would be revisited by grotesque images of his mother and sister. When he was painting however, he was able to look at his models and could import aspects of his traumatic memories into his work without being overwhelmed by them. Through painting, he was in control of the images before him. Munch's art operated as a function of transitional phenomena, allowing him to deal with reality by sufficiently altering it with personal meaning.

Munch's paintings of women served a purpose similar to that of the two-year-old's bath water tea ceremony. Both overcame trauma by transforming it. For Munch, the process of painting and the paintings themselves provided essential emotional security. In fact, when Munch painted he often surrounded himself with completed portraits — a social gathering subject to his control. This "community" of portraits helped him adapt to social interaction in the real world by connecting internal and external reality. Through the use of illusion, he was able to mediate trauma and engage more fully in the external world.

As "tea" was to the two-year-old boy, painting was to Munch. Their explorations with transitional phenomena were bridges to the world, just as the child's blanket or the toddler's game are spans that connect outer experience to inner personal meaning, facilitating development and psychological health.

Art and Transitional Space

⌇ The example of Munch highlights the relationship of art to transitional space. Art exists as something real and external and also expresses the projected meanings of the artist. There is a direct developmental line from the teddy bear of childhood to the creativity of adult life. The artist employs his or her personal, idiosyncratic psychology and transforms it into a book, painting, photograph, movie, etc. The work then becomes something public, onto which others project their own meanings. In a Winnicottian view, such an artistic creation, like a child's's transitional object, is both "me" and "not-me," containing all of the child's or artist's subjectivity and being squarely embedded in objective reality. It is simultaneously discovered in the outside world and created by the artist, a phenomenon Michelangelo allegedly once described when he characterized sculpting as the process of removing those portions of a block of stone that concealed the intended figure.

Whereas imagination evolves from interactive response between an individual's inner and outer life, in Winnicott's schema, fantasy is the product of an individual's reactivity to a chronically impinging environment. It is a defense that is dissociated and therefore unavailable to the individual for further enrichment and integration of reality states. In fantasy, contents are sequestered, separating internal experience and external reality rather than connecting or integrating them. The problem that this dissociative defense presents is that it forces an individual to experience internal fantasy and external reality as completely separate and disconnected. Fantasy cannot enrich everyday living because it is experienced as a refuge or retreat from the real, external environment. In fantasizing, there is no bridge, no transitional space to provide and make possible the integration of internal reality and external experience. Dissociated from experience, fantasizing attempts to protect a diminished sense of self from increased futility and hopelessness.[55] Fantasizing is organized to protect a vulnerable self from experiencing both prohibited aspects of internal reality such as rage, depression, envy, or pride, and painful aspects of the external world. Dent elaborated on the use of fantasy resulting from "… a sudden breakdown of the maternal holding environment, which was previously available and reliable. Infants in these circumstances have begun to discover their capacity for imagination, but their ability to play with this capacity is cut off prematurely. They develop a reactive rather than spontaneous relationship to outer reality, and in a self-protective maneuver wall off their true imaginative potential from the public "self" who maintains relations with the impinging outside world."[56]

This observation is certainly apt in thinking about Anaïs's early trauma and how it affected her later relationships and artistic endeavors. Experiencing severe illness in early childhood interfered with her safe, predictable, spontaneous relationship to the external world, as did the chaos and violence imposed on her by her parents' relationship. Though Anaïs's capacities for empathy and intuition were forged in this environment, so were her difficulties in maintaining a sense of independent creativity, security, and continuity in her relationships. Of necessity, Anaïs learned to be hypervigilant because her earliest experiences in the world were so unpredictable and fraught with physical and emotional pain. While fantasy protects the self from further environmental slights or assaults, the extent to which it is sequestered from the dialectical process between inner and outer experience may imbue it with the quality of an addiction or a fetish. The salient characteristics of both addiction (action) and fetish (substance) express a repetitive and concrete need that cannot be symbolically fulfilled.

SUSPENSION SPACE

⌘ Exploring Anaïs's diary-writing on the continuum from transitional object to fetish object, in engagement with or foreclosure of potential space, there exists another possible way to think about what, how, and why she wrote. This explanation is the notion of suspension space. Rather than sharing the continuum of transitional / fetish development, suspension space runs perpendicular to it, offering a unique means of thinking about creative development and expression.

Imagine the moment just after a child has fallen down. For an instant, perhaps only a few seconds, there is silence. Sometimes the silence is simply shock, quickly followed by a scream of fear, pain, or need for attention. Other times, this silence represents something else: the child is assessing whether or not he or she is okay, whether or not he or she should cry or continue playing. In this situation, the child has not yet assigned a meaning to the event. He or she does not yet know whether it is a crisis, a comedy, or something in between. Its significance hangs in the balance. The experience is not ambiguous. It simply does not yet have a name. This moment can be referred to as suspension space. It is the hypothetical moment before meaning is assigned to an experience, memory, or perception.

When a sculptor evaluates a block of stone, an artist confronts a blank canvass, a writer stares at an empty page, a composer sits at the keyboard, he or she is momentarily in suspension space. Meaning has not yet been assigned to the task, though intention is present. Suspension space may temporarily precipitate a retreat if the artist is daunted by the prospect of imbuing his or her world with meaning at that moment. Or it may result in creative work being accomplished.

Anaïs once alluded to this experience when she said that when she felt blocked, she could remediate the situation by swimming. The water refreshed not only her body, but her creative flow, enabling her to return to the process of writing without interference from her critical mind. She could allow the meaning that was present but unconscious to inform the process again.[57] Another example of suspension space is the moment described earlier in "The Miracle

Worker" before Helen assigns meaning to the water flowing over her hand.

Suspension space can best be understood as an action rather than a state of being. It is the dynamic by which an artist does not know what he or she will paint until the painting is completed; the composer cannot imagine the music until he or she plays it on the keyboard; the writer does not know what he or she thinks until the words appear on the paper or computer screen. Meaning is assigned by virtue of the process of doing. It is not attributed until the action is completed. Suspension space, brief or attenuated, is familiar to all who confront their own creativity. It is a space of possibility.

THE DIARY OF ANAÏS NIN

~ The words "Dear Diary" evoke numerous images. Depending on our experience of journal-writing or journal-reading, this invocation conjures Henry David Thoreau, Anne Frank, Anaïs Nin, a loved one long departed, or, perhaps ourselves. This salutation can introduce a travelogue, a mystery, a war story, a birth, a death, a deception. Maintaining a diary, a record of daily life is a form of communication whose meaning is imparted by the conscious and unconscious dynamics of its author. A diary is always part of a relationship, though it can serve numerous functions for any given author. Exploring the history and psychological uses of this relationship broadens our understanding of how keeping a diary functions to promote or obstruct psychological well-being, encourage or impede a flourishing interface between internal and external reality, and guide us towards or away from our goals and desires.

Anaïs, herself, best describes this dynamic:

> In the world of the dreamer there was solitude: all the
> exaltations and joys came in the moment of preparation
> for living. They took place in solitude. But with action
> came anxiety, and the sense of insuperable effort
> made to match the dream, and with it came weariness,
> discouragement, and the flight into solitude again. And
> then in solitude, in the opium den of remembrance,
> the possibility of pleasure again.[58]

Most often, a diary functions as a transitional object,
expressing both the personal psychology of the diarist, and
functioning as a bridge to the outside world. Sometimes that
world is evident in that the diarist intends for the diary to be
seen, either because it contains socially useful information
or because the diarist has a need to reveal him or herself to
others. Sometimes the role of the outside world is more subtle,
evident only in the fact that the diarist is writing his or her
thoughts down in a form that is potentially accessible to others.
The diary is always an intermediate form of communication.
It can be extremely candid, or, as it was for Anaïs, highly
sculpted and edited. It can be concealed, or made available
to be read. In Anaïs's case, it was both.

Diaries of the sort that Anaïs kept have all the markings
of the transitional object. As the toddler did with his bath
water and Munch did with his painting, Anaïs did with her
diary and diary-writing to master the trauma of her father's
abandonment, her mother's fragility, and her struggle with
self-esteem. She used her diary as a highly sophisticated

fairy tale to pretend to herself and to others that she was penitent, moral, honest, creative, desirable, intelligent, and uninhibited. This is not to say that she was not, at times, all of the these things in reality. The diary provided her with just the right format with which to deal with her traumatic experiences by constructing a story of her life that was both realistic and fantastic.

Because of the diary's privacy, Anaïs disclosed her feelings without the shame she carried much of the time. She also attempted to resolve this shame by reworking her feelings, perceptions, and memories in ways that restored her sense of creativity and self-esteem. This process is evident in the way she re-wrote the story of her arrival by boat in New York Harbor, an event that took place shortly after she began her diary and that marked the beginning of her new life in America. In the first account, she writes simply and concretely:

August 12 [1914]

Yesterday we reached New York. It was hot and humid, the thunder rumbled, and on account of the fog we had to wait between the entrance to the port and the dock. A heavy rain began to fall, there was thunder and finally lightning. All the Spaniards fell on their knees and prayed. All that finished and about eight o'clock we started up again and twenty minutes later we were in New York.[59]

This account, though a factual and relatively detailed observation, is flat. It records the event, but in a way that restricts the exploration of internal experience. This passage simultaneously denies and exposes the unthinkable, in this case, the reality of separation from Anaïs's father and an unknown future. This entry lacks personal meaning, the critical ingredient that would give it a vital, transitional quality. Following, is the revision, recorded nearly seven months later, on April 1, 1915. Anaïs prefaces it by stating, "I am thinking of rewriting my arrival in New York because the account that is in my diary is badly done and not my real thoughts." [60]

The elapsed time is significant and suggests that Anaïs needed sufficient distance from the event to titrate her initial emotions and make use of her diary to process the experience:

> We were all dressed and on deck. It was 2 o'clock and one could vaguely see a city, but very far away. The sea was gray and heavy. How different from the beautiful sea of Spain! I was anxious to arrive, but I was sad. I felt a chill around my heart and I was seeing things all wrong.

> Suddenly we were wrapped in a thick fog. A torrential rain began to fall, thunder rumbled, lightning flashes lit the heavy black sky. The people promptly took refuge in the lounge. None of the Spanish passengers had ever seen weather like that, so the frightened women wept, the men prayed in low tones. We were not afraid. Maman had seen many other storms and her calmness reassured us. We were the first to go back up on the wet deck. But the fog continued and we waited.

It was 4 o'clock when the ship began to move again, slowly, as though she approached the great city with fear.[61]

This second entry expresses in symbolic and metaphoric intensity the emotional quality of this experience. It evokes the complex layers of feelings that arriving on a foreign shore have conjured for an eleven-year-old. The revision involves Anaïs's imagination as mediator between reality and her internal experience, helping her integrate a traumatic event by transforming it through the use of symbol and metaphor. Here, Anaïs uses language and the form that her diary offers to master a trauma and create an adaptive illusion. The diary, as a dynamic of transitional phenomena offered her a way out of the trap of factual, depressive reality.

At other times, however, the diary seemed to foreclose Anaïs's creativity. It was as if its transitional function broke down and ceased to provide a context in which she could resolve trauma and promote imagination. Though her diary enabled Anaïs to make contact with her tremendous creative energy, her psychological difficulties at times were significant enough to inhibit the free expression of this energy. Anaïs's depression, her constant struggle with guilt and low self-esteem often made use of her diaries as transitional objects difficult. Because she needed to create a fictional account of who she really was, embroider reality to ward off feelings of shame and guilt, her diaries sometimes lost their transitional quality. They certainly never emboldened her to develop her art in the public direction in which she desired to go. In some ways, Anaïs's diaries helped her move forward in her life, master trauma, and live more creatively. They also facilitated a solipsistic world of self-aggrandizement and self-dramatization that interfered with her creative expression in the real world. Diary-writing is as complex and multi-layered as any intimate relationship. Similar to such relationships, it too provides the possibility of disappointment, and the opportunity for continued fulfillment.

Sometimes, solutions to problems become problems themselves: the child cannot give up the blanket, play by other people's rules, or relinquish omnipotent control in order to deal with social reality. In these cases, illusion becomes fantasy, even delusion. Diary-writing, too, can lose its adaptive properties. What begins as a means to an end can become an end in itself: a refuge from and denial of the real world rather than a way to engage more fully with it.

Anaïs's diary served both dynamics. She enlivened her trip to New York and comforted what must have been a tormented and grief-stricken soul. She wrote about sexual fantasies and liaisons in ways that helped her become less sexually inhibited. She experimented with self-dramatization as a prelude to her attempts at more creative interaction in the public world. She also, however, recounted such pathological experiences as her affairs with her analysts, cousin, and especially her father, simultaneous marriages to two husbands, her third trimester abortion, and her almost continual lying and subterfuge, without any mature awareness of how disturbed she was and how much psychic pain she must have been in to be compelled to such extremes. Instead, these accounts were sanitized, even idealized, first in the initial writing and then in the eventual publication. At these moments, Anaïs used her diary to foreclose exploration of her inner experience, seeking instead to make her life a work of art. In this effort, the transitional functions of the diary collapsed and Anaïs retreated into a kind of omnipotence that the diaries, like all transitional objects, are originally intended to transcend.

Notes: Part v – Dear Diary

1. Fothergill, R., 1974, p. 20.
2. Ibid., p. 20.
3. Mallon,T., 1984, p. 1.
4. Ibid., p. 34.
5. Ibid., p. 119.
6. Nin, A., 1978, p.233.
7. Fitch, N.R., 1993, p. 54.
8. Boxer, S., 1991, p. 20.
9. Mallon, T., 1984, p. 209.
10. Nin, A., 1978, p. 63.
11. Mallon, T., 1984, 251.
12. Ibid., p. 63.
13. Blos, P., 1967, p. 162.
14. Ibid., p. 162.
15. Nin, A., 1978, p. 65.
16. Ibid., p. 39.
17. Dalsimer, K., 1982, p. 519.
18. Ibid., p. 519
19. Ibid., p. 529.
20. Greenberg, J.R., & Mitchell, S.A., 1983, p. 190.
21. Winnicott, D.W., 1971d, p. 69.
22. Winnicott, D.W., 1965c, pp. 53-54.
23. Winnicott, D.W., 1965f, p. 223.
24. Winnicott, D.W., 1971a, p. 12.
25. Winnicott, D.W., 1971d, p. 62.
26. Grolnick, S., 1990, p. 30.
27. Winnicott, D.W., 1971a, p. 11.

28. Winnicott, D.W., 1971a, p. 11.
29. Ibid., p.12.
30. Ibid., p. 5.
31. Bair, D., 1995, p. 24.
32. Winnicott, D.W., 1971a, p. 3.
33. Ogden, T., 1986, p. 203.
34. Dent, V., 1990, p. 22.
35. Ogden, T., 1986, p. 214.
36. Freud, S., 1927/1961.
37. McDougall, J., 1989, p. 82.
38. Bronstein, A., 1992, p. 256.
39. Ibid., p. 257.
40. Ogden, T., 1986, p. 211.
41. Winnicott, D.W., 1965a.
42. Ibid.
43. Benjamin, J., 1988, p. 38.
44. Ibid.
45. Ibid., p. 40.
46. Ibid., p. 36
47. Winnicott, D.W., 1968, pp. 86-94.
48. Winnicott, D.W., 1971d, p. 65.
49. Ibid.
50. Winnicott, D.W., 1965a, p. 146.
51. Winnicott, D.W., 1975, pp. 182-183.
52. Winnicott, D.W., 1965d, p. 148.
53. Winnicott, D.W., 1971d, p. 68.
54. Ogden, T., 1986, pp. 206-207.
55. Dent, V., 1990, p. 26.
56. Ibid.
57. Nin, A., 1972, personal communication.

58. Nin, A., 1959, pp. 92-93.
59. Nin, A., 1978, p. 12.
60. Ibid., p. 57.
61. Ibid.

Appendix A: Works by Anaïs Nin

Fiction

Nin, A. *The House of Incest*. Paris: Siana Editions, 1936.

Nin, A. *The Winter of Artifice*. Paris: The Obelisk Press, 1939.

Nin. A. *Winter of Artifice*. New York: Gemor Press, 1942; Denver: Swallow, revised edition, 1961.

Nin, A. *Under a Glass Bell*. New York: Gemor Press, 1944; New York: E.P. Dutton, 1948.

Nin, A. *This Hunger*, (Part I of *Ladders to Fire*, 1946). New York: Gemor Press, 1945.

Nin, A. *Ladders to Fire*. New York: E. P. Dutton, 1946; Denver: Swallow Press, 1966.

Nin, A. *The All-Seeing*. (Chapbook). New York: Gemor Press, 1944.

Nin, A. *A Child Born Out of the Fog*. (Pamphlet). New York: Gemor Press, 1947.

Nin, A. *House of Incest*. New York: Gemor Press, 1947; Denver: Swallow Press, 1958.

Nin, A. *Children of the Albatross*. New York: E. P. Dutton, 1947; Denver: Swallow Press, 1966; Swallow Press/Ohio University Press: Athens, 1959.

Nin, A. *The Four Chambered Heart*. New York: Duell, Sloan and Pearce, 1950; Denver: Swallow Press, 1966.

Nin, A. *Auletris*. Carmel, California: Press of the Sunken Eye, 1950.

Nin, A. *A Spy in the House of Love*. New York: British Book Centre, 1954; Denver: Swallow Press, 1966.

Nin, A. *Solar Barque*. New York: Anaïs Nin, 1958.

Nin A. *Cities of the Interior*. (*Ladders to Fire, Children of the Albatross, The Four-Chambered Heart, Seduction of the Minotaur*). Denver: Swallow Press,

232

1974; Chicago: Swallow Press, 1959.

Nin, A. *Seduction of the Minotaur*. Denver: Swallow Press, 1961.

Nin, A. *Collages*. Denver: Swallow Press, 1964.

Nin, A. *The Anaïs Nin Reader*. (Ed. Philip K. Jason). Chicago: Swallow Press, 1973.

Non Fiction

Nin, A. "The Mystic of Sex," *The Canadian Forum,* October, 1930.

Nin, A. *D.H. Lawrence: An Unprofessional Study*. Paris: Edward W. Titus 1964; Denver: Swallow Press, 1932.

Nin, A. *The Novel of the Future*. New York: Macmillan, 1968.

Nin, A. *An Interview with Anaïs Nin*. Athens, Ohio: Duane Schneider, 1970.

Nin, A. *Nuances*. Cambridge: Sans Souci Press, 1970.

Nin, A. *A Woman Speaks: The Lectures, Seminars and Interviews of Anaïs Nin*. (Ed. Evelyn Hinz). Chicago: Swallow Press, 1975.

Nin, A. *In Favor of the Sensitive Man, and other Essays*. New York: Harcourt Brace Jovanovich, 1976.

Nin, A. *Delta of Venus: Erotica*. New York: Harcourt Brace Jovanovich, 1977.

Nin, A. *Little Birds: Erotica*. New York: Harcourt Brace Jovanovich, 1979.

Nin, A. *The White Blackbird and Other Writings*. Santa Barbara: Capra Press, 1985.

APPENDIX B: WORKS ABOUT ANAÏS NIN

FILMS

Ritual in Transfigured Time, Maya Deren, director. 1946.

Inauguration of the Pleasure Dome, Kenneth Anger, director. 1950.

Bells of Atlantis, Ian Hugo, director. 1952.

Jazz of Lights, Ian Hugo, director. 1954.

Melodic Inversion, Ian Hugo, director. 1958.

Through the Magicscope, Ian Hugo, director. 1968.

The Henry Miller Odyssey, Robert Snyder, director. 1969.

Aertura, Ian Hugo, director. 1970.

Henry and June. Philip Kaufman, director. Feature film, based on Anaïs Nin's diary. 1991.

AUDIO RECORDINGS

Anaïs Nin, Contemporary Classics. Sound Portraits. Louis and Bebe Barron. 1949.

The Diary of Anaïs Nin, Volume One: 1931-1934. Spoken Arts, SA995, SA996. 1968.

Anaïs Nin Observed: Portrait of a Woman as Artist. Robert Snyder, director. Documentary, 60 minutes. 1974.

Anaïs Nin in Recital: Diary Excerpts and Comments. Caedmon. 1979.

234

REFERENCES

Bair, D. *Anaïs Nin, a Biography*. New York: G. P. Putnam's Sons, 1995.

Benjamin, J. *The Bonds of Love*. New York: Pantheon Books, 1988.

Bion, W.R. *Learning From Experience*. London: William Heinemann, 1962.

Blos, P. *On Adolescence: A Psychoanalytic Interpretation*. New York: The Free Press, 1962.

Blos, P. "The second individuation process of adolescence." *Psychoanalytic Study of the Child*, 1967. Pages 22, 162-186.

Blos, P. "The Function of the Ego Ideal in Late Adolescence." *Psychoanalytic Study of the Child*, 1972. Pages 27, 93-97.

Boxer, S. E. *A Private Space: An Object-relations Analysis of Keeping a Diary.* Unpublished doctoral dissertation, Wright Institute, Berkeley, California, 1991.

Bronstein, A. "The Fetish, Transitional Objects, and Illusion." *Psychoanalytic Review*, 1992. Pages 79 (2), 139-260.

Dalsimer, K. "Female Adolescent Development: A Study of the Diary of Anne Frank." *Psychoanalytic Study of the Child*, 1982. Pages 37, 487-522.

Dent, V. *Personality Orientation and Literary Experience.* Unpublished doctoral dissertation, Wright Institute, Berkeley, California, 1990.

Evans, I. (Ed.). *Brewer's Dictionary of Phrase & Fable.* New York: Harper & Row, 1981.

Fitch, N. R. *Anaïs: The Erotic Life of Anaïs Nin.* New York: Little, Brown and Company, 1993.

Fothergill, R. *Private Chronicles: A Study of English Diaries.* London: Oxford University Press, 1974.

Freud, S. The aetiology of hysteria. In J. Strachey (Ed. and Trans.), *The Standard Edition of the Complete Psychological Works of Sigmund Freud* (Vol.

3, pp. 27-254). London: Hogarth Press, 1961. (Original work published 1896.)

Freud, S. "The Ego and the Id." In J. Strachey (Ed. and Trans.) *The Standard Edition of the Complete Psychological Works of Sigmund Freud* (Vol. 19, pp. 19-39). London: Hogarth Press, 1961. (Original work published 1923.)

Freud, S. "Fetishism." In J. Strachey (Ed. and Trans.), *The Standard Edition of the Complete Psychological Works of Sigmund Freud* (Vol. 21, pp. 149-157). London: Hogarth Press, 1961. (Original work published 1927.)

Gilligan, C. *In a Different Voice: Psychological Theory and Women's Development.* Cambridge, Massachusetts: Harvard University Press, 1982.

Green, A. "The Double and the Absent." In A. Roland (Ed.), *Psychoanalysis, Creativity, and Literature: A French-American Inquiry.* New York: Columbia University Press, 1978. (Original work published 1973.)

Greenacre, P. "The Transitional Object and the Fetish: With Special Reference to the Role of Illusion." In *Emotional Growth: Psychoanalytic Studies of the Gifted and a Great Variety of Other Individuals* (Vol. 1). New York: International Universities Press, 1970.

Greenberg, J. R., & Mitchell, S. A. *Object Relations in Psychoanalytic Theory.* Cambridge, MA: Harvard University Press, 1983.

Grolnick, S. *The Work and Play of Winnicott.* Northvale, N. J.: Jason Aronson, 1990.

Grotstein, J. S. "Winnicott's Importance in Psychoanalysis." In M. G. Fromm & B. L. Smith (Eds.), *The Facilitating Environment.* New York: International Universities Press, 1989.

Herman, J. *Trauma and Recovery.* New York: Basic Books, 1992.

Hinz, E. *The Mirror and the Garden: Realism and Reality in the Writings of Anaïs Nin.* New York: Harcourt Brace Jovanovich, 1973.

Jong, E. *The Devil at Large: Erica Jong on Henry Miller.* New York: Turtle Bay, 1993.

Mallon, T. *A Book of One's Own: People and Their Diaries*. New York: Ticknor & Fields, 1984.

McDougall, J. *Theaters of the Mind*. New York: Basic Books, Inc., 1985.

McDougall, J. *Theaters of the Body*. New York: W. W. Norton & Company, 1989.

Miller, A. *Thou Shalt Not be Aware: Society's Betrayal of the Child*. (H. Hannum & H. Hannum, Trans.). New York: Farrar, Straus & Giroux, 1984.

Nin, A. *Winter of Artifice*. Denver: Alan Swallow, 1945. (Originally published 1939.)

Nin, A. *Children of the Albatross*. Chicago: The Swallow Press, 1959.

Nin, A. *The Diary of Anaïs Nin (1931-1934)*. New York: The Swallow Press, and Harcourt, Brace & World, 1966.

Nin, A. *The Diary of Anaïs Nin (1934-1939)*. New York: The Swallow Press, and Harcourt, Brace & World, 1967.

Nin, A. *The Diary of Anaïs Nin, Volume Three: (1939-1944)*. New York: Harcourt, Brace & World, 1969.

Nin, A. *Linotte, the Early Diary of Anaïs Nin: 1914-1920*. New York: Harcourt Brace Jovanovich, 1978.

Nin, A. *The Early Diary of Anaïs Nin, Volume Two: (1920-1923)*. New York: Harcourt Brace Jovanovich, 1982.

Nin, A. *The Early Diary of Anaïs Nin, Volume Three: (1923-1927)*. New York: Harcourt Brace Jovanovich, 1983.

Nin, A. *The Early Diary of Anaïs Nin, Volume Four: (1927-1931)*. New York: Harcourt Brace Jovanovich, 1985.

Nin, A. *Henry and June, From the Unexpurgated Diary of Anaïs Nin*. New York: Harcourt Brace Jovanovich, 1986.

Nin, A. *Incest, From a Journal of Love*. New York: Harcourt Brace Jovanovich, 1992.

Ogden, T. H. *The Matrix of the Mind: Object Relations and the Psychoanalytic Dialogue*. Northvale, New Jersey: Jason Aronson, 1986.

237

Rainer, T. *The New Diary*. Los Angeles: Jeremy P. Tarcher, 1978.

Roiphe, H. & Galenson, E. *Infantile Origins of Sexual Identity*. New York: International Universities Press, 1981.

Stuhlmann, G., (Ed.). *A Literate Passion: Letters of Anaïs Nin & Henry Miller, 1932-1953*. New York: Harcourt Brace Jovanovich, 1987.

Wallerstein, J. *Second Chances: Men, Women, and Children a Decade after Divorce*. New York: Ticknor and Fields, 1989.

Webster, M. (Ed.). *Webster's New Collegiate Dictionary* (2nd ed.). Springfield, Massachusetts: G. & C. Merriam Co., 1960.

Winnicott, D.W. "Paediatrics and Psychiatry." In *Through Paediatrics to Psycho-Analysis* (157-173). New York: Basic Books, 1975. (1948.)

Winnicott, D.W. "Transitional Objects and Transitional Phenomena." In *Playing and Reality* (pp. 1-25). New York: Basic Books, 1971. (1951.)

Winnicott, D.W. "Psychosis and Child Care." In *Through Paediatrics to Psycho-Analysis* (pp. 219-228). New York: Basic Books, 1975. (1952.)

Winnicott, D.W. "Primary Maternal Preoccupation." In *Collected Papers: Through Paediatrics to Psycho-Analysis*. London: Tavistock Publications, 1958. (1956.)

Winnicott, D.W. "The Capacity to be Alone." In *The Maturational Processes and the Facilitating Environment*. (Pp. 29-36). New York: International Universities Press, 1965. (1958.)

Winnicott, D.W. "The Theory of the Parent-infant Relationship." In *The Maturational Processes and the Facilitating Environment*. (pp. 37-55). New York: International Universities Press, 1965. (1960.)

Winnicott, D. W. "The Capacity to be Alone." In *The Maturational Processes and the Facilitating Environment* (pp. 29-36). London: Hogarth Press, 1965a. (Originally published 1958.)

Winnicott, D. W. "The Theory of the Parent-infant Relationship." In The Maturational Processes and the Facilitating Environment (pp. 37-55). London: Hogarth Press, 1965b. (Originally published 1960.)

238

Winnicott, D. W. "Ego Integration in Child Development." In *The Maturational Processes and the Facilitating Environment* (pp. 56-63). London: Hogarth Press, 1965c. (Originally published 1962.)

Winnicott, D.W. "Ego Distortion in Terms of the True and False Self." In *The Maturational Processes and the Facilitating Environment* (pp. 140-152). London: Hogarth Press, 1965d. (Originally published 1960.)

Winnicott, D. W. "Communicating and not Communicating Leading to a Study of Certain Opposites." In *The Maturational Processes and the Facilitating Environment* (pp. 179-192). London: Hogarth Press, 1965e. (Originally published 1963.)

Winnicott, D. W. "The Mentally Ill in your Case Load." In *The Maturational Processes and the Facilitating Environment* (pp. 217-229). London: Hogarth Press, 1965f. (Originally published 1963.)

Winnicott, D.W. "The Use of the Object and Relating Through Cross Identifications." In *Playing and Reality* (pp. 86-94). New York: Basic Books, 1971. (1968.)

Winnicott, D. W. "Transitional Objects and Transitional Phenomena." In *Playing and Reality* (pp. 1-25). London: Tavistock Publications, 1971a.(Originally published 1953.)

Winnicott, D. W. "Dreaming, Fantasying, and Living: A Case-history Describing a Primary Dissociation." In *Playing and Reality* (pp. 26-37). London: Tavistock Publications, 1971b.

Winnicott, D. W. "Playing: Creative Activity and the Search for the Self." In *Playing and Reality* (pp. 53-64). London: Tavistock Publications, 1971c.

Winnicott, D. W. "Creativity and its Origins." In *Playing and Reality* (pp. 65-85). London: Tavistock Publications, 1971d.

Winnicott, D. W. "The Use of an Object and Relating Through Identifications." In *Playing and Reality* pp. 86-94). London: Tavistock Publications, 1971e.(Originally published 1969.)

Winnicott, D. W. "The Location of Cultural Experience." In *Playing and Reality* (pp. 95-103). London: Tavistock Publications, 1971f. (Originally published 1967.)

Winnicott, D. W. *Through Paediatrics to Psycho-Analysis.* New York: Basic Books, 1975.

Author photograph: Terry Lorant

About the Author

～ Margot Duxler is a licensed clinical psychologist in private practice in San Francisco, California. She has also worked as a professional musician and freelance writer. Her previous publications include the short stories, "All the Time in the World," "Before it Happened," "Bright Colors," "Constellations," "Marie's Wedding," and "Music." She served as co-editor of fiction for the *Five Fingers Review*, and co-translator for the first edition of the Gault-Millau's *The Best of Paris*. She is currently working on a novel and a collection of short stories.

EDGE
WORK

EDGEWORK BOOKS began like this: a room full of writers — women, most in their fifties. Some had written best-sellers. Some were poets, most were therapists, or teachers of some kind. And all of them, once they started comparing notes, were worried about the shape and direction of the publishing industry. More and more, the really hot books were being turned down as "brilliant but too literary," "too feminist," "too unusual" to compete for market share. If this was happening to them, at the peak of successful careers, what was happening to the voices of emerging women writers? Who was encouraging, publishing, distributing, and marketing their best work?

EdgeWork Books began when this room full of women said, "We've got to have viable alternatives to the New York publishing machine," and one of them responded, "Well, if not us, then who?"

So that's us. We're trying to be the press we've been waiting for. We want to be part of the decentralization and democratization of the publishing industry — the structures that support it, the people who run it, and the work it produces. We publish well-written books with fresh artistic vision and, through our Web site, we offer supportive writing classes, individual writing consultation, coaching, editing, and open forums.

Please come join us — we look forward to meeting you online: **www.edgework.com**